# SICILIA

# EATING IN SICILY

## THE CANDOUR OF THE COMMON PEOPLE
## AND THE GENTEELNESS
## OF THE ARISTOCRACY
## IN A CUISINE EVOCATIVE OF THE SUN,
## SEA, PASTURES AND CITIES OF SICILY

**BONECHI**

# HOW TO READ THE CARDS

| DIFFICULTY | FLAVOUR | NUTRITIONAL VALUE |
|---|---|---|
| ● Simple | ● Mild | ● Low |
| ●● Moderat | ●● Moderately spicy | ●● Medium |
| ●●● Difficult | ●●● Spicy | ●●● High |

Preparation and cooking times are shown in hours (h) and minutes (e. g. 30′ is 30 minutes).

Project and editorial concept: Casa Editrice Bonechi
Series editor: Alberto Andreini
Coordinator: Paolo Piazzesi
Graphic design: Andrea Agnorelli
Layout: Vanni Berti
Cover: Maria Rosanna Malagrinò
Edited by: Patrizia Chirichigno
Translation: Stephanie Johnson

Chef: Lisa Mugnai
Nutritionist: Dr. John Luke Hili

The photograph on the cover is the property of the Bonechi Archives
and was taken by Paolo Giambone.

The photographs in the cover flaps were taken by
Andrea Fantauzzo, Paolo Giambone, Francesco Giannoni, Pier Silvio Ongaro.

The photographs of the dishes are the property of the Bonechi Archives
and were taken by Andrea Fantauzzo.
The photographs of the dishes on pp. 13, 16, 26, 52, 54, 56, 60, 104, 116, 117, and
124 are the property of the Bonechi Archives and were taken by Pier Silvio Ongaro.

The landscape photographs are the property of the Casa Editrice Bonechi Archives
and were taken by: Paolo Abbate (at the top page 3, top left page 4, page 8),
Andrea Fantauzzo (top left and bottom right page 3,
top centre and top right page 4, top page 5, page 28)
Paolo Giambone (p. 68), Pier Silvio Ongaro (bottom p. 5),
Giuliano Valsecchi (p. 43).
The landscape photographs on pages 3 (bottom) and 4 (bottom left)
are reproduced by the kind concession of Francesco Giannoni.

For the photographs with no identified source, the Editor would appreciate any
information to enable their integration in reprinted editions.

ISBN 88-476-0311-0

# INTRODUCTION

Sicilian cooking is indeed rich, with such a variety of dishes that elaborate, complex delicacies are offered alongside dishes of a simplicity inversely proportional to their excellence.

For anyone broaching a presentation of these culinary delights, inevitably one calls to mind the multiple influences of the different civilisations, with often contrasting customs, which have succeeded each other in the island, leaving an indelible imprint on her culture. Following a proven

*Palermo: an elegant sconce on the Palazzo dei Normanni. Above: opulent decoration and colour on a typical Sicilian cartwheel.*

scenario in the Mediterranean basin, Greeks and Romans, Byzantines and Arabs, Normans and Swedes, Angevins and Aragonese, attracted by the treasures of Trinacria (as the island was called by the ancient Greeks) have in turn enriched it with marvels that make it a jewel of unparalleled worth. But, whereas in the field of *objets d'art* and archaeological finds it is not difficult to pinpoint the matrix of traditions and customs with certainty from among the tangle of superimposition, manipulation and contamination, here in the realm of gastronomy it is, on the contrary, not easy. Apart from some rather superficial connections (olive oil and the Greeks, sweet-sour and the

*Palermo: detail of a fountain in Piazza Pretoria.*

*Palermo: scenes of the picturesque market of Vucciria.*

Arabs, for example), attempts to go back to the most recent origins of Sicilian cuisine often go no further than an assumption that is at times, quite frankly, absurd. That having been stated and given that it is not history which satisfies the appetite, we do not wish to get mixed up in acrobatic and brash hypotheses, but rather emphasise how so many influences have converged and stratified, following the mysterious alchemies of taste and the unfathomable logic of gastronomy. Thus, with the complicity of the sea and the sun, gardens crammed with vegetables, secular olive groves and amber-coloured vines, they have given rise to a culinary palette of matchless charm. Sicilian gastronomy is an outstanding certainty in the copious and articulated panorama of regional Italian and European cooking. The spread you find at the dinner table in the island is both lavish and humble, noble (the actual term is "baronial") and plebeian, solemn as in a patronal feast and simple like the daily bread. It is austere and substantial, without frills or decorations, like in the Syracuse and Ragusa districts, lands with an ancient agricultural tradition. It is refined, fanciful and tantalising for the eye as well as for the palate. An example is the cuisine in the Palermo district where excellent pastries triumph – for a long time they had been locked up in a convent where they were refined. You will indeed find Sicilian cuisine to be mouth-watering, aromatic, healthy (thanks to olive oil), inviting, unpredictable and suitable on any occasion.

# PREFATORY NOTE

*T*o facilitate the reader in working through our recipes, most of them are photographed, illustrating the steps. Salt and pepper are not usually included in the list of ingredients, as their culinary use in Italy goes without saying, just as water is needed for boiling pasta or other foodstuffs. Listing them would only waste time and space, but the moment they should be added to the dish is indicated in the recipe. Only among the ingredients for sweets and biscuits will salt be listed when necessary, because its use is occasional. Our advice is to go through the list of ingredients with care (the time necessary for the preparation and cooking of the dish is also given, as well as an indication of the level of difficulty and the intensity of flavour, whether more or less pronounced, together with the dietetical value), then to read each stage of the recipe carefully before starting out. And, as they say in Italy, "Buon appetito!"

## GLOSSARY

**Pecorino**: is a hard or semi-hard sheep's milk cheese and is available at varying stages of ripening.

**Ricotta**: made from ewe's milk, is soft and fresh, looking rather like cottage cheese.

**Caciocavallo**: is a mild or sharp hard cheese which is usually smoked.

**Toma**: unsalted cheese from cow's milk.

**Provola**: is a semi-hard cheese made from buffalo milk, eaten fresh or smoked.

**Primosale**: is a fresh, compact cheese.

**N.B.**: Liquid measures are given in litres, pints and American cups.

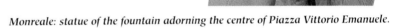

*Monreale: statue of the fountain adorning the centre of Piazza Vittorio Emanuele.*

# DIFFERENT TOWNS....
# DIFFERENT RECIPES

*Palermo: a triumph of colours (and flavours) in marzipan fruits, a speciality of Sicilian confectionary art.*

*I*n the cuisine of **Western Sicily**, juicy oranges are relished in salads, and bitter-sweet flavours are delicately balanced with care (such as in *Caponata*), but there are also straightforward and essential dishes, such as *Pasta a' carrittera*, Splish-Splash Pasta, Bucatini with Cauliflower, *Pasta fritta china* and *Ciciri ca pasta*. The sardine, a leading player in Sicilian cuisine, triumphs on **Palermo** tables and animates specialities such as *Pasta cu li sardi* and *Sardi a beccaficu* which, like *Farsumagru*, have spread throughout the whole island. Should you prefer white meat, you can opt for a tasty *Jadduzzu zogghiatu*, chicken in *Zogghiu*, a fragrant sauce based on mint, parsley, garlic, olive oil and vinegar. To round off, you can indulge yourself with magnificent temptations such as *Biancamanciari*, *Cannola* and *Cassata*, or you can nibble fruits made of *pastareale* (marzipan), based on the almonds from the beautiful trees sheltering so many parts of Sicily from the hot sun (especially in the **Ragusa** district).
Cous Cous gives a Maghribi air to the **Trapani** district, where in their

*Pasta ca buttarga* there is a taste of the sea, and an aroma of herbs in their *Pasta cu pistu trapanisi*. From the town of **Marsala** we get *Mataroccu* and the sophisticated *Arata ammarsalata*. In the **ancient core** of the island we find *Sfogghiu* in the Madonie Mountains, *Pasta ca ricotta* in Piazza Armerina (in the province of Enna) and *Cavatiddi cu sucu* at Caltanissetta. The Baked Sea Bream from Agrigento stands out among many delicacies on the southern coast, whilst *Sardi a chiappa*, *Trigghi 'n tianu* and that very delicate dessert *Minni di virgini* come from Sciacca. After welcoming us with the delicious *arancini*, **Eastern Sicily** also alternates humble dishes (*Pasta c'anciova*, *Pasta ca muddica*, *Tunnina ca cipuddata* and *Zippuli*) with very elaborate creations (*Tummàla di riso* and *Agneddu agglassatu*). The sword fish and the aubergine, another two main players on the stage of Sicilian gastronomy, hold their sway here and have spread throughout the island in the authentic, sumptuous *Piscispata arrustutu cu salamurigghiu* - an aromatic dressing made of oregano, lemon and olive oil - and the *Milinciani chini* resembling snuff boxes. **Messina** displays skill in cooking both fresh fish (*Piscispata a' missinisa*) and conserved fish (*Piscistoccu agghiotta* and *Piscistoccu chi milinciani*). The aubergine is a leading player in **Catania**, too, with *Pasta ca Norma*, so called in homage to Vincenzo Bellini and his best-known heroine, supported by *Pasta ca nnocca*, *Pasta cu niuru di sicci* and the delicious *Cunigghiu a' cacciatura*. Flavours become more pronounced at **Syracuse**, with the *Maccu di San Giuseppe* and the vinegar-based speciality *stimpirata* which is used to mask sword fish (*Piscispata a la stimpirata*) and rabbit (*Cunigghiu a la stimpirata*). Major cuisine for feast days triumphs at **Modica** at the New Year (*Lasagni di Capu d'annu*) and at carnival time (*Pignuccata*), while **Ragusa** responds with their superb *Pasta 'ncasciata* and the refined *Scaccia di maiali*. Indeed, feast days are a gastronomic jamboree all over Sicily, where Christmas is celebrated with *Pasticciu di sustanza* and Carnival with *Mustazzola* and *Ravioli di Carnalivari*.

# ADVICE FROM
# THE NUTRIZIONIST

We are at the heart of the Mediterranean Sea, in the reign of the Mediterranean diet, which shares characteristics with Greek, Arabic and Spanish cooking. To the fore is the fibre in vegetables; carbohydrates are offered in the form of bread, pasta, pulses (legumes); extra virgin olive oil is the prominent source of fats, mono-unsaturated fats in particular (to stave off arteriosclerosis); little resort is made to red meat, while widely used are white meats and particularly fish, prepared simply. All things considered, it offers an ideal healthy diet which the whole world is envious of, but which, in actual fact, we Sicilians ourselves do not manage to abide by completely.... Sicilian desserts are very good, but they are among the most laden of all regional cooking in Italy. While there is a frequent use of ricotta cheese (beyond all guilt), there is also a great quantity of candied fruit, chocolate, liqueurs, sugar, lard and fried foods....A note to end with: the nutritional assessment of each recipe takes into account the method of cooking it.

# INDEX OF RECIPES

*Palermo: view of the beach at Mondello.*

# APPETITERS AND SAUCES

1

# ALICI A L'ARANCI

Anchovies with Orange

800 g / 7 oz fresh anchovies
1 large orange, squeezed
150 g / 5 oz / 1 cup green olives
Dried bread crumbs
Hot red pepper
Pine nuts
Parsley
1 lemon
Dry white wine
Olive oil

| | |
|---|---|
| Servings: | 4 |
| Preparation time: | 15' |
| Cooking time: | 20' |
| Difficulty: | ● ● |
| Flavour: | ● ● |
| Kcal (per serving): | 726 |
| Proteins (per serving): | 43 |
| Fats (per serving): | 34 |
| Nutritional value: | ● ● ● |

Lightly toast a handful of dried bread crumbs in a pan. Bone the anchovies and discard the heads. Slice the lemon finely, chop the parsley and olives (stoned). Arrange a layer of anchovies in a glass oven dish and lay lemon slices on top. Sprinkle over some pine nuts, chopped parsley and pieces of hot red pepper and olives. Continue until all the ingredients are used up. Season carefully with salt. Drizzle over some olive oil and a glass (half a cup) of wine. Finish with a layer of bread crumbs and bake in the oven at 160-180 °C / 300-350°F / Gas Mark 2-4 for about twenty minutes. Halfway through cooking time, douse with the orange juice.

# ARANCINI DI RISU

## Rice Patties

| |
|---|
| 500 g / 1 lb 2 oz / 2 cups Italian rice |
| 3 eggs |
| Plain flour |
| Saffron |
| Grated pecorino cheese |
| 120 g / 4 oz firm cheese |
| Dried bread crumbs |
| Oil for frying |

*For the filling:*
Pre-prepared meat sauce
100 g / 4 oz / $^1/_2$ cup fresh, shelled peas
Dried mushrooms
Sage

| | |
|---|---|
| Servings: 6-8 | |
| Preparation time: 40′ | |
| Cooking time: 2h | |
| Difficulty: ● ● ● | |
| Flavour: ● ● ● | |
| Kcal (per serving): 929 | |
| Proteins (per serving): 31 | |
| Fats (per serving): 50 | |
| Nutritional value: ● ● ● | |

Boil the rice in lightly-salted water until just tender. Drain and heap up on a work surface. Work in a handful of pecorino cheese, half a sachet of saffron dissolved in 4 tablespoons of hot water and 2 beaten eggs. Meanwhile, separately heat some meat sauce, together with the blanched peas and the mushrooms (previously moistened and squeezed). Adjust for salt and add a twig of sage and slowly blend the flavours.

1 In the palm of your hand, shape a quantity of rice the size of half an orange, hollowing it out in the middle, and fill with a little of the meat sauce.

2 Add the diced pasty cheese, seal off the "orange" with some more rice and mould into shape. Be careful not to let the filling spill out.

3 Roll the *arancini* in flour, then in the one remaining beaten egg and then bread crumbs. Fry until golden with plenty of boiling oil (or lard). Drain on kitchen paper and keep warm.

# BACCALARU FRITTU

Fried Salt Cod

800 g / 1³/₄ lb salt cod, soaked
3-4 ripe tomatoes
1 clove of garlic
Flour
Oregano
Olive oil
Oil for frying

| | |
|---|---|
| Servings: | 4 |
| Preparation time: | 20' |
| Cooking time: | 35' |
| Difficulty: | ● ● |
| Flavour: | ● ● ● |
| Kcal (per serving): | 605 |
| Proteins (per serving): | 54 |
| Fats (per serving): | 35 |
| Nutritional value: | ● ● ● |

Cut the salt cod into reasonably-sized chunks, coat lightly in flour and fry in plenty of boiling oil, taking care that the pieces colour all over. Drain and season cautiously with salt. Clean, seed and roughly chop the tomatoes and put in a saucepan with 2-3 tablespoons of olive oil, a pinch of salt and pepper, a handful of oregano and the finely-chopped garlic. Leave to simmer. Serve the fried *baccalà* very hot with the tomato sauce.

800 g / 1 $^3/_4$ lb cauliflower
2 eggs
Flour
Anchovy paste
Oil for frying

| | |
|---|---|
| Servings: 4 | |
| Preparation time: 20' | |
| Cooking time: 35' | |
| Difficulty: ● ● | |
| Flavour: ● ● | |
| Kcal (per serving): 439 | |
| Proteins (per serving): 17 | |
| Fats (per serving): 31 | |
| Nutritional value: ● ● ● | |

# BROCCULI A PASTETTA

Cauliflower Fritters

Blanch the cauliflower in plenty of lightly salted water, drain and divide into bite-sized pieces. Beat the eggs in a bowl, sprinkle in the flour and whisk until there are no lumps. Finally, mix in a teaspoon of anchovy paste.
Coat the cauliflower pieces in the batter, leaving them in the bowl for a few minutes. Fry in plenty of boiling hot oil. Season with salt and serve them nice and crisp.

# CAPONATA

Aubergine Stew

Clean and slice the aubergines (eggplant). Place on a tray, sprinkle with coarse salt and leave under a weight for about an hour until the bitter liquid runs out. Meanwhile, trim the celery and blanch in lightly-salted water for five minutes. Drain, cut into chunks and brown gently in a little oil in a frying pan. Set aside.

1 Peel the onion, slice finely and let it colour in 3-4 tablespoons of oil in a frying pan, together with the rinsed capers, the olives and a handful of pine nuts. Add the skinned, seeded tomatoes, cut to pieces. Blend the flavours over gentle heat (20 min.).

2 Rinse, dry and dice the aubergines. Brown in 4-5 tablespoons of boiling oil in the frying pan. As soon as they turn golden, toss in the celery and the onion and tomato sauce.

3 Stir over a gentle flame (20 minutes), adjusting the salt. Add a teaspoon of sugar and the vinegar. Allow to evaporate. Garnish with a sprig of basil and leave to cool before serving. *Caponata* will keep in the refrigerator for a few days.

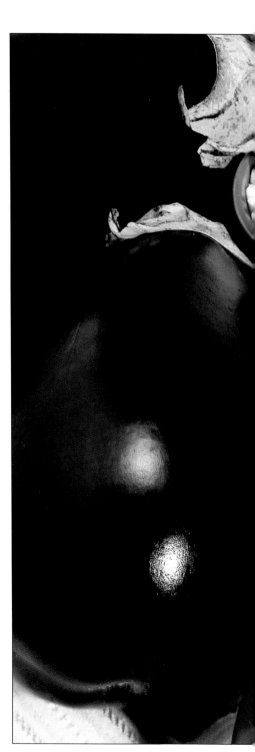

| | | Servings: 4-6 |
|---|---|---|
| 800 g / 1³/₄ lb aubergines (eggplant) | Pine nuts | Preparation time: 40' +1 h |
| 3 celery stalks | Granulated sugar | Cooking time: 1 h 15' |
| 2 onions | Vinegar, a liqueur glass | Difficulty: ● ● ● |
| 2-3 tomatoes | Olive oil | Flavour: ● ● ● |
| 120 g / 4 oz / ³/₄ cup green olives, stoned | | Kcal (per serving): 389 |
| Fresh basil | | Proteins (per serving): 9 |
| Capers | | Fats (per serving): 29 |
| | | Nutritional value: ● ● ● |

# CARDUNA IN PASTETTA

Batter-fried Cardoons

4 cardoons
1 egg
10 g / $^1/_4$ oz fresh brewer's
    yeast or 2 tsp active dry yeast
Plain flour
Anchovy paste
Oil for frying

| | |
|---|---|
| Servings: | 4 |
| Preparation time: | 20'+20' |
| Cooking time: | 25' |
| Difficulty: | ●● |
| Flavour: | ●●● |
| Kcal (per serving): | 333 |
| Proteins (per serving): | 4 |
| Fats (per serving): | 27 |
| Nutritional value: | ●●● |

Clean and trim the cardoons. Blanch in slightly-salted water, drain and cut into even-sized lengths. Make a thick batter by dissolving 6-7 tablespoons of flour in a scant glass (scant half cup) of warm water which the yeast has already been dissolved in. Work in the beaten egg, a teaspoon of anchovy paste and leave to rest for about twenty minutes. Coat the cardoon pieces in batter and fry in plenty of boiling oil in a frying pan. Drain, season cautiously with salt and serve nice and crisp.

# COZZULI GRATINÉ

## Mussels au Gratin

Toast a handful of bread crumbs lightly in a frying pan. Skin, seed and dice the tomatoes and fry in 4-5 tablespoons of oil, together with a pinch of salt and a sprig of basil (15 minutes). Chop the garlic with some parsley. Scrub, rinse and beard the mussels. Allow them to open in a frying pan over fierce heat and reserve their liquor, after filtering it. Separate the shells into two halves and discard the empty ones. Lay the halves containing a mollusc in a glass oven dish, masking each one in the tomato sauce. Sprinkle over the garlic, parsley and dried bread crumbs. Then douse the mussels with a little of the reserved liquor, mixed with a drop of olive oil, and season with salt and pepper. Place in a pre-heated oven at 180 °C / 350°F / Gas Mark 4 and cook for 5-6 minutes. Sprinkle half a glass (a quarter cup) of wine over the mussels, dust with fresh oregano and bake for another 6 minutes.

1-1.2 kg / 2¹/₄ lb-2 lb 10 oz mussels
3-4 ripe tomatoes
2 cloves of garlic
Fresh basil, oregano, parsley
Dried bread crumbs
Dry white wine
Olive oil

| | |
|---|---|
| Servings: 4 | |
| Preparation time: 30' | |
| Cooking time: 15' | |
| Difficulty: ● ● | |
| Flavour: ● ● | |
| Kcal (per serving): 267 | |
| Proteins (per serving): 12 | |
| Fats (per serving): 12 | |
| Nutritional value: ● ● ● | |

## CRISPEDDI

Dumplings of Ricotta and Anchovy

600-700 g / 1 lb 5 oz-1¹/₂ lb/
  6-7 cups durum semolina
180 g / 6 oz / 1 scant cup
  fresh, sieved sheep's ricotta
  cheese
3-4 salted anchovies
25 g / 1oz / 2 tbsp fresh
  brewer's yeast or 5 tsp active
  dry yeast
Oil (or lard) for frying

Servings: 4
Preparation time: 40'+3 h
Cooking time: 20'
Difficulty: ● ●
Flavour: ● ●
Kcal (per serving): 957
Proteins (per serving): 25
Fats (per serving): 41
Nutritional value: ● ● ●

Work the semolina with lightly-salted hot water and the yeast in a bowl to make a smooth, fluid dough. Cover the bowl with a cloth and leave to rest for 3 hours. Rinse and bone the anchovies and cut to pieces.
Heat plenty of oil (or lard) in a capacious frying pan. Take a nut-sized piece of dough and fill with a strip of anchovy or a spoonful of ricotta, differing the shape according to the filling. Fry the *crispeddi* until they turn a nice golden colour. Remove with a slotted spoon and drain on kitchen paper. Season carefully with salt. The secret? On filling and shaping the dough, your hands should always be damp, so that your fingers do not stick together. Serve the *crispeddi* crisp.

# GAMMAREDDI SPIZZUSI

## Piquant Shrimps

Skin and seed the tomatoes and chop roughly. Rinse the shrimps and parboil in slightly-salted, boiling water. Drain and reserve. Slice the onion finely, soften in a pan with 3-4 tablespoons of oil and the crushed garlic. Discard the latter after 2-3 minutes. Add a generous soup ladle (4 tbs.) of tomato sauce and a pinch of salt and allow to reduce over a gentle flame (6-8 minutes). Add the tomatoes in pieces, a sprig of roughly-chopped parsley, the shrimps and a little hot red pepper, checking the salt. Sauté briskly for 7-8 minutes and serve.

600 g / 1 lb 5 oz shrimp tails
2-3 cherry tomatoes
Freshly-made tomato sauce
Half an onion
1 clove of garlic
Fresh parsley
Hot red pepper
Olive oil

| | |
|---|---|
| Servings: 4 | |
| Preparation time: 30' | |
| Cooking time: 25' | |
| Difficulty: ●● | |
| Flavour: ●● | |
| Kcal (per serving): 228 | |
| Proteins (per serving): 23 | |
| Fats (per serving): 13 | |
| Nutritional value: ●●● | |

# MILINCIANI CHINI

## Stuffed Aubergines (Eggplant)

4-5 aubergines (eggplant)
or 8, if small
1 onion
50 g / 2 oz salami
2 egg whites
2 cloves of garlic
2-3 salted anchovies
Salted capers
Dried bread crumbs
Parsley
Olive oil
Oil for frying

| | |
|---|---|
| Servings: 4 | |
| Preparation time: 45' | |
| Cooking time: 30' | |
| Difficulty: ● ● ● | |
| Flavour: ● ● ● | |
| Kcal (per serving): 500 | |
| Proteins (per serving): 14 | |
| Fats (per serving): 42 | |
| Nutritional value: ● ● ● | |

1 Trim the aubergines and cut into halves. Parboil them in salted water, draining while they are still firm to the bite. Scoop out the flesh, taking care not to break the skins, and keep aside. Toast a handful of bread crumbs in a frying pan.

2 Slice the onion and soften in 3-4 table-spoons of olive oil a frying pan. Toss in the aubergine pulp and a pinch of salt and let the flavours blend.

3 Add the capers, the rinsed and filleted anchovies, the garlic and parsley chopped up together and pieces of the salami. Stir, allow the flavours to marry well, add the bread crumbs and draw off the heat.

4 Stuff the aubergines with the mixture and seal them with more of the bread crumbs, previously moistened in the beaten egg white. Place (cut-side down) in a frying pan and fry in plenty of boiling oil. Turn over and fry the other side, too.

450 g / 1 lb / 3 cups plain
  flour
20 g / ¹/₂ oz fresh brewer's
  yeast or 4 tsp active dry yeast
200 g / 7 oz stewing veal
100 g / 3 ¹/₂ oz stewing pork
1 onion
Toasted almonds
2 egg whites, plus 1 yolk
30 g / 1 oz plain (bitter)
  chocolate
Granulated sugar
Lard, olive oil

| | |
|---|---|
| Servings: 4 | |
| Preparation time: 50'+1 h | |
| Cooking time: 1 h | |
| Difficulty: ● ● ● | |
| Flavour: ● ● ● | |
| Kcal (per serving): 1110 | |
| Proteins (per serving): 40 | |
| Fats (per serving): 58 | |
| Nutritional value: ● ● ● | |

# L'MPANATIGGHIA

Focaccia (Flat Bread)

Prepare a dough with the flour, yeast, a drop of water and a little lard (or oil). Leave for about an hour to rise. Slice the onion, colour slightly with 3-4 tablespoons of oil in a pan and then brown the veal and pork in it. After 8-10 minutes, melt the plain chocolate in the same pan and add the toasted, finely-chopped almonds. Dust with sugar and season with salt and pepper. At the end of cooking, chop up the mixture and blend in the 2 egg whites. Roll the dough out into two rounds of different sizes. Use the bigger one to line a greased tin. Spoon over the filling up to 2 cm from the edge. Level it off and seal with the smaller disc. Prick over the surface, after brushing it with the beaten egg yolk. Bake in the oven at 200 °C / 400°F / Gas Mark 6. Remove the 'mpanatigghia when it is a nice golden colour and serve.

# 'NZALATA CAVALERA

## Shellfish Salad

C lean the tomatoes and cut into wedges. Hard boil the eggs (7 minutes). Rinse the shell fish, parboil in lightly-salted water for a few minutes and drain. Prise out the flesh and cut into pieces. Place in a bowl with a tablespoon of capers and a sprig of chopped parsley. Dress with olive oil, salt, pepper and the juice of a lemon. Arrange the shellfish salad in the centre of a serving dish, garnishing with wedges of tomato and hard-boiled egg. Chill for about an hour in the refrigerator before serving.

300 g / 11 oz lobster
300 g / 11 oz prawns
4-5 ripe tomatoes
2 eggs
1 lemon
Capers
Fresh parsley
Olive oil

| | |
|---|---|
| Servings: 4 | |
| Preparation time: 20' | |
| Cooking time: 6' | |
| Difficulty: ● | |
| Flavour: ● | |
| Kcal (per serving): 415 | |
| Proteins (per serving): 26 | |
| Fats (per serving): 17 | |
| Nutritional value: ● ● ● | |

23

# PIPI CHINI

## Stuffed Peppers

1 Slice the onion and brown with the chopped parsley in 4-5 tablespoons of oil in a frying pan.
After 4-5 minutes, draw off the heat and toss in enough bread crumbs to absorb all the oil.

2 Allow to cool. Add pecorino and the garlic with a sprig of parsley, all chopped up, and the rinsed anchovies, cut to pieces. Make sure that the mixture is not too solid. Check for salt and pepper.

3 Slice off the top of the peppers and eliminate the white pith and the seeds. Stuff the peppers to the brim.

4 Dip the open end in the beaten egg and in the bread crumbs. Place the peppers face down in plenty of boiling oil in a frying pan and fry until a golden crust has formed across the filling. Then lower the flame and continue cooking on all sides.

4 sweet peppers
1 onion
1 clove of garlic
2-3 salted anchovies
1 egg
100 g / 4 oz / ³/₄ cup pecorino
    cheese with peppercorns, grated
Parsley
Dried bread crumbs

Olive oil
Oil for frying

| | |
|---|---|
| Servings: 4 | |
| Preparation time: 40' | |
| Cooking time: 20' | |
| Difficulty: ● ● ● | |
| Flavour: ● ● ● | |
| Kcal (per serving): 518 | |
| Proteins (per serving): 15 | |
| Fats (per serving): 45 | |
| Nutritional value: ● ● ● | |

# PURPU VUGGHIUTU

Octopus Salad

800 g / 1³/₄ lb octopus
1 lemon
1 shallot (scallion)
Green olives
Parsley
Olive oil

| | |
|---|---|
| Servings: 4 | |
| Preparation time: 20'+30' | |
| Cooking time: 1 h + 20' | |
| Difficulty: ● | |
| Flavour: ● ● ● | |
| Kcal (per serving): 307 | |
| Proteins (per serving): 22 | |
| Fats (per serving): 22 | |
| Nutritional value: ● ● ● | |

Clean and trim the octopus. Boil in salted water, leaving it to cool in its stock. Drain, cut into pieces and transfer to a bowl. Dress with oil, salt, chopped parsley and lemon. Add the onion, roughly chopped, and a handful of stoned olives. Chill the salad in the refrigerator for half an hour before serving it.

# SPITINI DI MARI

Seafood Skewers

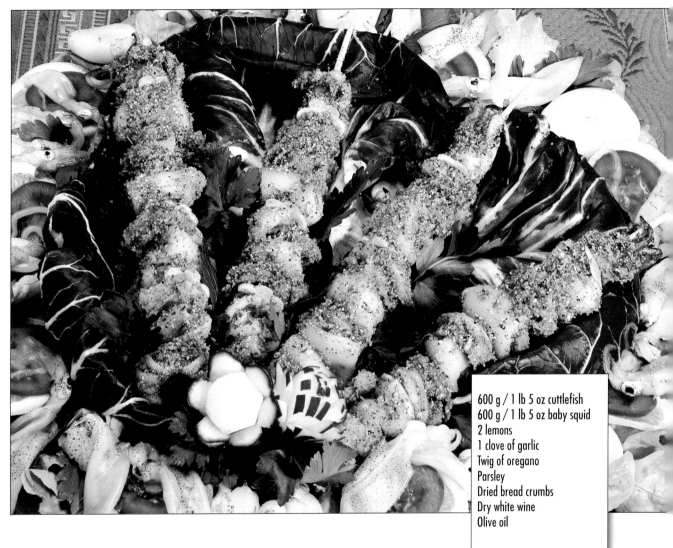

600 g / 1 lb 5 oz cuttlefish
600 g / 1 lb 5 oz baby squid
2 lemons
1 clove of garlic
Twig of oregano
Parsley
Dried bread crumbs
Dry white wine
Olive oil

| | |
|---|---|
| Servings: 4 | |
| Preparation time: 20' | |
| Cooking time: 15' | |
| Difficulty: ● | |
| Flavour: ● ● | |
| Kcal (per serving): 395 | |
| Proteins (per serving): 42 | |
| Fats (per serving): 15 | |
| Nutritional value: ● ● ● | |

Clean the shellfish under running water, discarding any cartilage and the small ink sacs. Toast a generous handful of bread crumbs and mix with chopped garlic and parsley in a bowl. Coat the shellfish thoroughly in the crumb mixture and dress with salt, pepper, a trickle of oil and half a glass (a quarter cup) of wine. Thread the cuttlefish and squid onto skewers, alternating them with slices of lemon. Grill (broil) over blazing charcoal or under an electric grill, using a twig of oregano to brush the skewers with oil which has been seasoned with salt and pepper. Turn the skewers over from time to time.

*Monreale: the artistic fountain in Piazza Vittorio Emanuele.*

# MATAROCCU

## Sicilian Pesto

Although traditionally a wooden pestle was used, take advantage of an electric blender to chop a fair-sized bunch of fresh basil, a sprig of parsley, a handful of pine nuts, the garlic, celery leaves and the tomatoes, cut into pieces. Put the mash in a bowl and gradually mix in a full glass (half-cup) of oil.

Just like the pesto sauce from Liguria, *mataroccu* is ideal in pasta dishes, for lending flavour to vegetable soups or for serving with small batter-fried fish.

Fresh basil
Parsley
2-3 tomatoes
Leafy celery
3 heads of garlic
Pine nuts
Olive oil

| | |
|---|---|
| Servings: 4 | |
| Preparation time: 20' | |
| Difficulty: ● | |
| Flavour: ● ● ● | |
| Kcal (per serving): 316 | |
| Proteins (per serving): 8 | |
| Fats (per serving): 27 | |
| Nutritional value: ● ● ● | |

# SAMMURIGGHIU

## Oregano Sauce

2 cloves of garlic
2 lemons
Fresh oregano
Parsley
Olive oil

| | |
|---|---|
| Servings: 4 | |
| Preparation time: 20′ | |
| Cooking time: 10′ | |
| Difficulty: ● | |
| Flavour: ● ● | |
| Kcal (per serving): 144 | |
| Proteins (per serving): 1 | |
| Fats (per serving): 15 | |
| Nutritional value: ● | |

1 Pour a glass (half-cup) of oil into a saucepan. Add half a glass of hot water and the juice of a lemon, a little at a time, beating it all in with a fork or metal whisk. Season with salt and pepper. Then add a full table-spoon of fresh oregano, a small bunch of chopped parsley and the crushed garlic.

*Mazara del Vallo:*
*the ship-way harbour.*

**2** Simmer the sauce in a bain-marie (water bath) for 8-10 minutes. Transfer to a warmed dish and take to the dinner table. It is ideal to accompany baked fish. If you prefer something richer, amalgamate (at stage 1) the pulp of 2-3 grilled tomatoes from which the seeds have been removed and which have been blended in the electric blender.

# SARSA D'AMMAREDDI

Shrimp Sauce

350 g / ³/₄ lb shrimps
100 g puréed tomatoes
Ground hot red pepper
Dry white wine
Olive oil

| | |
|---|---|
| Servings: 4 | |
| Preparation time: 15' | |
| Cooking time: 15' | |
| Difficulty: ● | |
| Flavour: ● ● | |
| Kcal (per serving): 289 | |
| Proteins (per serving): 14 | |
| Fats (per serving): 17 | |
| Nutritional value: ● ● ● | |

Briefly scald the shrimps in lightly-salted boiling water and shell them (depending on your taste, if the shrimps are very fresh, you can crush the shells to a pulp and add to the sauce). Simmer the puréed tomato in a saucepan with 3-4 tablespoons of oil, a pinch of salt and a quarter of a spoon of hot red pepper. Add the shrimps after about ten minutes, douse with a few drops of wine and reduce the sauce until thick. It is excellent when served with poached fish.

# SARSA DI MENTA

Mint Sauce

Fresh mint
Vinegar
Olive oil

| | |
|---|---|
| Servings: 4 | |
| Preparation time: 10'+1 h | |
| Difficulty: ● | |
| Flavour: ●● | |
| Kcal (per serving): 127 | |
| Proteins (per serving): 0 | |
| Fats (per serving): 10 | |
| Nutritional value: ● | |

*This is very good
if used as a complement
to boiled meats.
It must be prepared
at least an hour
before needed.*

Chop a good-sized bunch of very fresh mint leaves. Energetically beat 3-4 tablespoons of olive oil into 2 tablespoons of vinegar in a bowl. Season with salt and pepper, then add the mint leaves. Stir carefully with a wooden spoon for at least 5 minutes. Allow the sauce to rest.

# ZOGGHIU

## Mint and Parsley Sauce

Fresh mint
Parsley
2 cloves of garlic
Vinegar
Olive oil

| | |
|---|---|
| Servings: 4 | |
| Preparation time: 20' | |
| Difficulty: ● | |
| Flavour: ● ● | |
| Kcal (per serving): 127 | |
| Proteins (per serving): 0 | |
| Fats (per serving): 10 | |
| Nutritional value: ● | |

Place an ample bunch of fresh mint leaves, a sprig of parsley and the garlic in the bowl of an electric blender and reduce to a pulp on a low speed. Transfer to a bowl where you will amalgamate a few drops of vinegar and a scant glass (half-cup) of olive oil, little by little, using a wooden spoon.
The sauce should be thick and smooth. It is perfect with grilled fish or white roast meat.

# Soups, Pasta and Rice Dishes

2

# CICIRI CA PASTA

Pasta with Chick Peas (Garbanzos)

500 g / 1 lb 2 oz chick peas
   (garbanzos)
300 g / 11 oz large ditali
   (thimble-sized pasta)
1 rasher (80 g / 3 oz) smoked
   streaky bacon
Freshly-made tomato sauce
   (optional)
Fresh chives, rosemary, sage
Hot red pepper
Olive oil

| | |
|---|---|
| Servings: 4 | |
| Preparation time: 15'+5-6 h | |
| Cooking time: 1 h 15' | |
| Difficulty: ● ● | |
| Flavour: ● ● | |
| Kcal (per serving): 1179 | |
| Proteins (per serving): 76 | |
| Fats (per serving): 46 | |
| Nutritional value: ● ● ● | |

1 Put the chick peas to soak 5-6 hours previously. Brown the diced bacon in a saucepan with 5-6 tablespoons of oil, a leaf of sage, a few rosemary needles, a little chopped chive and half a hot red pepper, broken up. If you like, add 4 generous tablespoons of tomato sauce.

2 Boil the chick peas in plenty of salted water and drain. Reserve the cooking water for boiling the pasta in. When the pasta is cooked *al dente*, draw off the heat but do not drain, add the chick peas with the bacon sauce and stir. Serve the dish nice and hot.

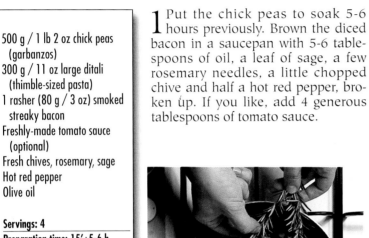

# CUSCUSÙ TRAPANISI

## Couscous Trapani Style

S crub and clean the fish and place in a pan where two chopped cloves of garlic and a onion have been browned in 3-4 tablespoons of oil. Dust with chopped parsley and cover with 2 litres (3½ pints / 9 cups) of hot water. Season with salt and pepper and simmer for 20 minutes. Remove from direct heat, but keep the fish warm. Place the couscous in a bowl and dress with 3-4 tablespoons oil, salt and pepper, and the remaining onion and garlic, all chopped up. Douse with the fish stock, but do not use up all of it. Cover the bowl with a cloth and keep warm for half-an-hour. Pour some more of the stock onto the couscous (which has swollen in the meantime) and stir. Divide among the dinner bowls, add some pieces of fish, douse again with the hot fish stock and season with a pinch of pepper.

1 kg / 2 ¹/₄ lb selection of fish
(eels, shellfish and a small
lobster)
200 g / 7 oz pre-cooked
couscous
4 cloves of garlic
2 small onions
Parsley
Olive oil

| | |
|---|---|
| Servings: 4 | |
| Preparation time: 30'+20' | |
| Cooking time: 20' | |
| Difficulty: ● ● | |
| Flavour: ● ● ● | |
| Kcal (per serving): 817 | |
| Proteins (per serving): 31 | |
| Fats (per serving): 34 | |
| Nutritional value: ● ● | |

# FAVATA

## Hot Broad Bean Salad

400 g / 14 oz dried broad beans
80 g / 3 oz smoked streaky bacon (one rasher)
80 g / 3 oz sausage
1 onion
Puréed tomatoes
Leaves of wild fennel
Slices of continental bread
Olive oil

| | |
|---|---|
| Servings: 4 | |
| Preparation time: 10'+5-6 h | |
| Cooking time: 1 h 10' | |
| Difficulty: ● ● | |
| Flavour: ● ● | |
| Kcal (per serving): 838 | |
| Proteins (per serving): 39 | |
| Fats (per serving): 21 | |
| Nutritional value: ● ● ● | |

S oak the broad beans for 5-6 hours before starting. Finely chop the onion and soften with the diced bacon in 3-4 tablespoons of oil in a pan. Stir in the wild fennel leaves and 4 tablespoons of tomato purée. Add the drained beans and the crumbled sausage, adjusting salt and pepper. Cook briskly, now and again adding a little warm water. Serve with slices of toasted bread.

# MACCU DI SAN GNUSEPPI

San Giuseppe Soup

200 g / 7 oz dried broad beans
100 g / 4 oz dried peas
100 g / 4 oz chick peas
100 g / 4 oz dried beans
100 g / 4 oz continental lentils
1 onion
2 dried tomatoes
2 bunches borrage
Fennel seeds
Wild fennel leaves
Slices of continental bread
Olive oil

| | |
|---|---|
| Servings: | 6 |
| Preparation time: | 10'+5-6 h |
| Cooking time: | 2 h |
| Difficulty: | ● |
| Flavour: | ● ● |
| Kcal (per serving): | 433 |
| Proteins (per serving): | 9 |
| Fats (per serving): | 16 |
| Nutritional value: | ● ● |

Put all the pulses (legumes), except the lentils, to soak separately for 5-6 hours. Drain and put them, together with the lentils, in a capacious saucepan. Cover with cold, salted water. Simmer with the lid on for a couple of hours. Half-way through cooking, add the sliced onion, the borage, a pinch of fennel seeds, a sprig of wild fennel leaves and the roughly-chopped tomatoes. When everything is ready, check the seasoning of salt and pepper. Dress in olive oil and serve with cubes of golden bread.

# PANICOTTU

## Bread Soup

400 g / 14 oz stale bread
4-5 ripe tomatoes
2 cloves of garlic
Parsley
Olive oil

| | |
|---|---|
| Servings: | 4 |
| Preparation time: | 10' |
| Cooking time: | 15' |
| Difficulty: | ● ● |
| Flavour: | ● ● |
| Kcal (per serving): | 387 |
| Proteins (per serving): | 9 |
| Fats (per serving): | 11 |
| Nutritional value: | ● ● |

1 Skin and seed the tomatoes and cut into pieces. Lightly brown the crushed cloves of garlic, together with a sprig of parsley in 4-5 tablespoons of oil in a saucepan. Then add the tomatoes.

2 Cover copiously with water, adjust the salt and, when it starts to boil, add the chunks of bread. Stir and cook over fierce heat for a few minutes to blend the flavours. Draw off the heat and flavour the soup with a little oil.

# PASTA CA FASOLA

Beans and Pasta

300 g / 11 oz tagliatelle
Half a white cauliflower
1 onion
500 g / 1 lb 2 oz borlotti beans
100 g / 4 oz pork rind
Olive oil

| | |
|---|---|
| Servings: | 4 |
| Preparation time: | 10'+5-6 h |
| Cooking time: | 1 h 30' |
| Difficulty: | ●● |
| Flavour: | ●● |
| Kcal (per serving): | 821 |
| Proteins (per serving): | 34 |
| Fats (per serving): | 32 |
| Nutritional value: | ●●● |

Put the beans to soak 5-6 hours before you start. Roughly chop the onion and soften it in 3-4 tablespoons of oil in a saucepan, where you will also brown the rinsed pork rind, broken up. Add the drained beans, cover copiously with water. Simmer with the lid on for a good hour, seasoning with salt and checking that there is always enough water. Add the trimmed cauliflower, cut into pieces. When it is cooked, but still firm to the bite, add the tagliatelle and cook *al dente*. Serve after drizzling over a little oil.

300 g / 11 oz / 3 cups
  semolina
Pre-prepared meat sauce,
  preferably including pork
Seasoned salt ricotta
  (or pecorino cheese),
  for grating

| | |
|---|---|
| Servings: 4 | |
| Preparation time: 30' | |
| Cooking time: 10' | |
| Difficulty: ●● | |
| Flavour: ●● | |
| Kcal (per serving): 553 | |
| Proteins (per serving): 24 | |
| Fats (per serving): 22 | |
| Nutritional value: ●● | |

# CAVATIDDI CU SUCU

Dumplings in Meat Sauce

Prepare the gnocchetti dumplings, mixing warm water into the semolina by hand. When the dough is soft and smooth, divide it into long breadsticks half-an-inch in diameter. Slice into inch-long lengths. Squash them with your thumb and lay them out to dry on a cloth.

Cook the gnocchi, removing them with a slotted spoon as they rise to the surface of the boiling water. Place in a bowl and toss in lots of meat sauce. Dust generously with grated cheese and serve immediately.

*View of the coastline at Aci Castello.*

# LASAGNI DI CAPU D'ANNU

New Year's Day Lasagne

1 Heap the flour into a "volcano" and break the eggs into the 'crater'. Work them in with a pinch of salt. Knead the dough energetically. Roll into a ball and leave to rest half an hour. Roll out thinly and cut into strips 1-1½in wide.

2 Cook the pasta *al dente*, removing the lasagne with a slotted spoon as soon as cooked. Transfer to a bowl with plenty of meat sauce. Dredge with lots of grated pecorino cheese. Place on a serving dish and cover with shavings of sieved ricotta cheese.

300 g / 11 oz / 2 cups plain flour
4 eggs
Pre-prepared meat sauce
150 g / 5 oz fresh ricotta cheese
Grated pecorino cheese

| | |
|---|---|
| Servings: | 4 |
| Preparation time: | 40'+30' |
| Cooking time: | 10' |
| Difficulty: | ● ● |
| Flavour: | ● ● ● |
| Kcal (per serving): | 816 |
| Proteins (per serving): | 35 |
| Fats (per serving): | 46 |
| Nutritional value: | ● ● ● |

# LINGUI DI PASSIRU CU RUNCU

Linguine with Conger Eel Sauce

350 g / ³/₄ lb linguine
  (ribbon pasta)
600 g / 1 lb 5 oz conger eel
  (or grey mullet)
3-4 ripe tomatoes
2 shallots (scallions)
1 clove of garlic
Parsley
Olive oil

| | |
|---|---|
| Servings: 4 | |
| Preparation time: 15′ | |
| Cooking time: 30′ | |
| Difficulty: ● ● | |
| Flavour: ● ● | |
| Kcal (per serving): 610 | |
| Proteins (per serving): 36 | |
| Fats (per serving): 21 | |
| Nutritional value: ● ● | |

Clean the fish and cut into rounds (or strips if it is mullet). Finely chop the onion and brown, together with the crushed garlic, in 3-4 tablespoons of oil in a saucepan. Remove the garlic, add the skinned and sliced tomatoes, adjusting the seasoning with salt and pepper. Add the fish after 10 minutes and allow it to absorb the flavours of the sauce slowly. Boil the pasta and drain when very much *al dente* (after four fifths of the cooking time). Transfer to the sauce in the casserole. Stir dust with chopped parsley and serve at the table.

# PASTA A' CARRITTERA

Spaghetti with a Piquant Sauce

350 g / ³/₄ lb spaghetti
(or bucatini - pasta straws)
4-5 ripe tomatoes
Fresh basil
2 cloves of garlic
Hot red pepper
Seasoned salt ricotta (or pecorino
cheese), to be grated
Olive oil

| | |
|---|---|
| Servings: 4 | |
| Preparation time: 15'+1 h | |
| Cooking time: 8' | |
| Difficulty: ● | |
| Flavour: ● ● | |
| Kcal (per serving): 507 | |
| Proteins (per serving): 18 | |
| Fats (per serving): 18 | |
| Nutritional value: ● ● | |

Wash, skin and seed the tomatoes and cut into pieces. Chop up the garlic finely and mix with plenty of basil leaves and the tomatoes in a bowl. Dress with olive oil, salt and chopped hot red pepper. Leave to stand for a good hour.
Cook the pasta and drain while still *al dente*. Add to the sauce and dust liberally with grated cheese. Serve immediately.

# PASTA A' MATALOTTA

Seafood Spaghetti

300 g / 11 oz spaghetti
(or spaghettini)
700 g / 1 ¹/₂ lb selection
of small fish (bass, grouper,
sea bream, etc.)
4-5 ripe tomatoes
1 onion
Parsley
Olive oil

| | |
|---|---|
| Servings: 4 | |
| Preparation time: 30' | |
| Cooking time: 20' | |
| Difficulty: ● ● | |
| Flavour: ● ● ● | |
| Kcal (per serving): 575 | |
| Proteins (per serving): 42 | |
| Fats (per serving): 18 | |
| Nutritional value: ● ● | |

Skin, seed and dice the tomatoes. Clean and trim the fish and cut into pieces. Slice the onion and brown in a frying pan with a sprig of parsley. Throw in the tomatoes and reduce slowly for 10 minutes. Add the fish, cover with water, season with salt and pepper, pour in a trickle of oil and cook briskly until the liquid has completely evaporated. Remove the fish and keep hot. Drain the cooked spaghetti while still *al dente* and pour the sauce over, keeping the fish aside for the main course.

# PASTA A PICCHI-PACCHIU

"Splish-Splash" Pasta

350 g / ³/₄ lb penne or sedani
  (fluted pasta tubes)
4 ripe tomatoes
1 onion
1 aubergine (eggplant)
1 clove of garlic
2-3 salted anchovies
Fresh basil
Olive oil

| | |
|---|---|
| Servings: 4 | |
| Preparation time: 30' | |
| Cooking time: 40' | |
| Difficulty: ●● | |
| Flavour: ●●● | |
| Kcal (per serving): 506 | |
| Proteins (per serving): 17 | |
| Fats (per serving): 18 | |
| Nutritional value: ●● | |

1 Slice the onion and soften, with the crushed garlic and a few basil leaves, in 3-4 tablespoons of oil in a frying pan. Add the skinned and seeded tomatoes, roughly chopped. Thicken the sauce over fierce heat, seasoning with salt and pepper.

2 Slice the aubergine and brown in 3-4 tablespoons of oil in the frying pan. Trim the anchovies and fillet them. Add both to the sauce, crushing the aubergine with a fork. In the meanwhile, boil the pasta and drain while still *al dente*. Dress with the sauce.

48

# PASTA CA BUTTARGA

## Spaghettini with Mullet Roes

W hile the pasta is cooking, brown the crushed garlic and the whole hot red pepper in 4-5 tablespoons of oil in a frying pan. As soon as the garlic begins to colour, remove it. Add the crumbled roes together with a sprig of parsley, finely chopped, and let the flavours blend over fierce heat for a couple of minutes.

Drain the spaghettini while just cooked but still firm to the bite and sauté briskly in the sauce in the frying pan for a moment. Draw off the heat as soon as it begins to sizzle.

350 g / ³/₄ lb spaghettini
  (thinner spaghetti)
150 g / 5 oz mullet roes
1 clove of garlic
Parsley
Hot red pepper
Olive oil

Servings: 4
Preparation time: 5'
Cooking time: 15'
Difficulty: ●
Flavour: ● ● ●
Kcal (per serving): 391
Proteins (per serving): 14
Fats (per serving): 13
Nutritional value: ● ●

# PASTA C'ANCIOVA E CA MUDDICA

Pasta with Anchovies and Dried Bread Crumbs

350 g / 3/4 lb reginette
  (ribbon pasta)
250 g / 9 oz feathery wild
  fennel leaves
5 salted anchovies
1 clove of garlic
Pine nuts
Sultanas
Parsley
Hot red pepper
Dried bread crumbs
Olive oil

| | |
|---|---|
| Servings: 4 | |
| Preparation time: 30' | |
| Cooking time: 20' | |
| Difficulty: ●● | |
| Flavour: ●●● | |
| Kcal (per serving): 740 | |
| Proteins (per serving): 25 | |
| Fats (per serving): 30 | |
| Nutritional value: ●●● | |

1 Steep a handful of sultanas in warm water. Colour the crushed garlic with a sprig of parsley in 3-4 tablespoons of oil in a frying pan. Remove both from the oil and dissolve the filleted anchovies in it, crushing them with a fork. Add a handful of pine nuts and the sultanas, squeezed of excess water.

2 Remove the sauce from the pan. Pour in a little oil and, over fierce heat, sauté a handful of bread crumbs, stirring. Blanch the fennel leaves in plenty of salted water. Then remove and boil the pasta to the *al dente* stage in the same cooking water. Toss in the sauce, the dried bread crumbs and the hot red pepper, broken up.

# PASTA CA NNOCCA

Pasta with Sardines and Peas

| | |
|---|---|
| 350 g / ³/₄ lb sedani (fluted pasta tubes) | |
| Half an onion, parsley | |
| 300 g / 11 oz fresh sardines (or sprats) | |
| 150 g / 5 oz / 1 half-cup shelled peas | |
| Olive oil | |

| | |
|---|---|
| Servings: 4 | |
| Preparation time: 15' | |
| Cooking time: 20' | |
| Difficulty: ● ● | |
| Flavour: ● ● | |
| Kcal (per serving): 276 | |
| Proteins (per serving): 10 | |
| Fats (per serving): 21 | |
| Nutritional value: ● ● | |

Sauté the sliced onion in 3-4 tablespoons of oil in a frying pan with the peas and a sprig of parsley, stirring. After 5-6 minutes, add the sardines, trimmed of the heads, bones and tails. Season with salt and pepper.
Cook the pasta. Drain while still firm to the bite and throw briefly into the pan with the sauce. Serve immediately.

# PASTA CA NORMA

Pasta alla Norma

Once sliced, the aubergines are to be sprinkled with coarse salt, placed under a weight and left for the juices to run out. Sauté the chopped onion, the crushed garlic and a few basil leaves in 4-5 tablespoons of oil in a saucepan. Toss in the tomatoes, roughly chopped, with a pinch of salt and reduce it all gently (15 minutes). Rinse the aubergine, dab dry and brown in 3-4 tablespoons of oil in a frying pan. Boil the spaghetti, drain *al dente* and stir into the tomato sauce, dredging with grated ricotta cheese. Add the aubergine, diced finely, a couple of basil leaves and another liberal sprinkling of cheese.

350 g / ³/₄ lb spaghetti
2 aubergines (eggplant)
4-5 ripe tomatoes
1 onion
2 cloves of garlic
Fresh basil
Seasoned ricotta or pecorino
   cheese (for grating)
Olive oil

| | |
|---|---|
| Servings: 4 | |
| Preparation time: 15'+30' | |
| Cooking time: 20' | |
| Difficulty: ● ● | |
| Flavour: ● ● | |
| Kcal (per serving): 584 | |
| Proteins (per serving): 31 | |
| Fats (per serving): 42 | |
| Nutritional value: ● ● | |

# PASTA CA RICOTTA

Pasta au Gratin

350 g / ³/₄ lb sedani
  (fluted pasta tubes)
250 g / 9 oz / 1¹/₄ cups fresh
  ewe ricotta cheese
Grated pecorino cheese
Powdered cinnamon
Olive oil

*To cook the meat:*
350 g / ³/₄ lb joint of chuck
  steak
1 onion, 1 clove
Bay leaf, cinnamon
Red wine

| | |
|---|---|
| **Servings:** | **4** |
| **Preparation time:** | **40'** |
| **Cooking time:** | **1 h 30'** |
| **Difficulty:** | ● ● |
| **Flavour:** | ● ● ● |
| **Kcal (per serving):** | **751** |
| **Proteins (per serving):** | **30** |
| **Fats (per serving):** | **28** |
| **Nutritional value:** | ● ● ● |

B rown the steak with the sliced onion in 3-4 tablespoons of oil in a saucepan. Douse with a glass (half a cup) of red wine, season with salt, one clove, a pinch of cinnamon and a bay leaf. Cover and leave to simmer for roughly an hour. When cooked, remove a cupful of the residue from the pan and blend into half of the ricotta, seasoning with salt and pepper.

Cook the pasta and drain after ⁴/₅ cooked. Transfer to an oiled ovenware dish. Dress with the ricotta-gravy mixture and a handful of grated cheese. Add shavings of the remaining ricotta and dust with the grated pecorino and a pinch of cinnamon. Bake in the oven at 200 °C / 400°F / Gas Mark 6 for 10 minutes. The steak can, of course, be eaten as the main course.

# PASTA CHI BROCCULI

Bucatini with Cauliflower

350 g / ¾ lb bucatini
  (pasta straws)
1 small cauliflower
1 onion
4-5 anchovy fillets
Pine nuts
Sultanas
Powdered saffron
Grated Parmesan cheese
Olive oil

| | |
|---|---|
| Servings: 4 | |
| Preparation time: 20'+30' | |
| Cooking time: 45' | |
| Difficulty: ● ● | |
| Flavour: ● ● ● | |
| Kcal (per serving): 564 | |
| Proteins (per serving): 20 | |
| Fats (per serving): 24 | |
| Nutritional value: ● ● | |

Soak the sultanas half-an-hour beforehand. Blanch the cauliflower in lightly-salted water. Drain and reserve the cooking water. Peel the onion and chop. Soften in 4-5 tablespoons of oil in a frying pan and add the anchovies, broken up. When the latter have dissolved, throw in the sultanas, squeezed of excess water, a handful of pine nuts and the tops of the cauliflower. Cook briskly for 10 minutes, stirring so that the cauliflower breaks up in the sauce. In the meantime, cook the pasta in the reserved cooking liquor. A moment before ready, dissolve a sachet of saffron in the water. Drain the bucatini while still very firm to the bite and sauté briefly in the frying pan. Serve dredged in grated Parmesan cheese (or mild provolone).

# PASTA CHI CUCUZZEDDI FRITTI

Spaghettini with Courgettes (Zucchini)

350 g / ³/₄ lb spaghettini
3-4 courgettes (zucchini)
1 clove of garlic
100 g / 4 oz peppered pecorino
cheese or salted ricotta
(for grating)
Olive oil

| | |
|---|---|
| Servings: 4 | |
| Preparation time: 10' | |
| Cooking time: 15' | |
| Difficulty: ● | |
| Flavour: ● ● | |
| Kcal (per serving): 850 | |
| Proteins (per serving): 46 | |
| Fats (per serving): 35 | |
| Nutritional value: ● ● ● | |

Trim the courgettes and slice into rounds. Fry the crushed garlic in 4-5 tablespoons of oil in a frying pan until golden. Remove and sauté the courgettes in the flavoured oil over fierce heat. Season with salt and pepper and keep warm.
Boil the spaghettini (finer spaghetti) and drain *al dente*. Dredge with lots of grated cheese, stir and dress with the courgettes in their cooking oil. Serve immediately. A simple, but delicious dish.

# PASTA CU LI SARDI

Pasta with Sardines

350 g / ³/₄ lb bucatini
   (pasta straws)
500-600 g / 1 lb 2 oz-1 lb
   5 oz fresh sardines (or sprats)
1 shallot (scallion)
Wild fennel tops
2 anchovies
Almonds, pine nuts, sultanas
Dried bread crumbs
Saffron
Olive oil

| | |
|---|---|
| Servings: 4 | |
| Preparation time: 10′ | |
| Cooking time: 15′ | |
| Difficulty: ● | |
| Flavour: ● ● | |
| Kcal (per serving): 929 | |
| Proteins (per serving): 49 | |
| Fats (per serving): 43 | |
| Nutritional value: ● ● ● | |

Soak a handful of sultanas in warm water. Toast a handful of skinned almonds in the oven and, in a frying pan, fry a generous handful of bread crumbs in a trickle of oil. Blanch a bunch of wild fennel leaves in plenty of salted water, keeping the water aside after draining the leaves. Clean the sardines, open them out flat and remove the heads and bones. Sauté the sliced onion together with the filleted sardines in 4-5 tablespoons of oil in the frying pan. When the sardines have dissolved, add the sultanas (squeezed of excess moisture), a tablespoon of pine nuts and a sachet of saffron. Season with salt, stir and allow the flavours to blend. Then add the chopped-up fennel tops and the sardines (keep 4 or 5 as a garnish). Boil the pasta in the water the fennel has been cooked in, adding a pinch of saffron. Drain while still firm to the bite, dress with the sauce and sprinkle with bread crumbs. Transfer to an oven dish, garnish with the whole sardines, chopped almonds and a trickle of oil. Bake in the oven at 200 °C / 44°F / Gas Mark 6 for 10 minutes.

# PASTA CU NIURU DI SICCI

Black Inkfish Spaghetti

C lean the cuttlefish, remove the bone (discard) and the ink-sacs (reserve). Sauté the sliced onion in 4-5 tablespoons of oil, together with a sprig of parsley, chopped. Add the cuttlefish, cut into strips, along with the roughly-chopped tomatoes. Cover and simmer gently (20 minutes). Take off the lid, add a couple of ink sacs and reduce the sauce. When the pasta is cooked, drain it *al dente* and sauté briefly in the black sauce in the frying pan. Dust with grated pecorino cheese and serve.

350 g / ³/₄ lb spaghettini
350 g / ³/₄ lb cuttlefish
1 onion
300 g / 11 oz tinned tomatoes
Parsley
Seasoned pecorino cheese
Olive oil

| | |
|---|---|
| Servings: 4 | |
| Preparation time: 15' | |
| Cooking time: 25' | |
| Difficulty: ● ● | |
| Flavour: ● ● | |
| Kcal (per serving): 567 | |
| Proteins (per serving): 30 | |
| Fats (per serving): 19 | |
| Nutritional value: ● ● | |

# PASTA FRITTA CHINA

Fried Stuffed Pasta

1 Blanch the sweet-breads (10 minutes) and rinse under cold water. Dice the ham. In 3-4 tablespoons of oil in a frying pan, sauté the chicken livers and hearts, the sweetbreads, the diced ham and the peas. Season with salt. Douse with half a glass (a quarter of a cup) of Marsala.

2 Cook the pasta. Drain while still firm to the bite and dress immediately with the butter and a handful of cheese.

58

| 500 g / 1 lb 2 oz capelli d'angelo (hair-fine pasta) 160 g / 5 ¹/₂ oz veal sweetbreads 120 g / 4 oz chicken hearts and livers 120 g / 4 oz / ¹/₂ cup shelled peas 30 g / 1 oz ham (in one rasher) | 2 eggs Dried bread crumbs Cinnamon Dry Marsala Grated pecorino cheese 50 g / 2 oz / 4 tbsp butter Olive oil |
|---|---|

| | |
|---|---|
| Servings: 6 | |
| Preparation time: 40'+10' | |
| Cooking time: 30' | |
| Difficulty: ● ● ● | |
| Flavour: ● ● ● | |
| Kcal (per serving): 1205 | |
| Proteins (per serving): 46 | |
| Fats (per serving): 54 | |
| Nutritional value: ● ● ● | |

3 Shape spoonfuls of pasta into nests and fill them with the sauce. Cover with some more pasta and seal into balls.

4 Dip in the egg, which has been beaten up with ground cinnamon and salt. Coat in bread crumbs, then fry in plenty of boiling hot oil until a golden crust has formed.

**3**

**4**

# PASTA CU PISTU TRAPANISI

Spaghetti Trapani-style

350 g / ³/₄ lb spaghetti
4-5 ripe tomatoes
1 clove of garlic
Fresh basil
Almonds, skinned
Grated pecorino cheese
Olive oil

| | |
|---|---|
| Servings: | 4 |
| Preparation time: | 10'+30' |
| Cooking time: | 12' |
| Difficulty: | ● |
| Flavour: | ● ● ● |
| Kcal (per serving): | 643 |
| Proteins (per serving): | 23 |
| Fats (per serving): | 29 |
| Nutritional value: | ● ● |

Skin and seed the tomatoes and dice them. Place in a bowl with a sprig of basil (chopped up with a handful of almonds), a trickle of oil and a handful of cheese. Set aside for half-an-hour.
Cook and drain the spaghetti *al dente*. Add to the bowl, stir and drizzle over a little more oil. Serve at once.

# Pasta 'Ncasciata

Pasta Pie

400 g / 14 oz fluted sedani (short pasta tubes)
100 g / 4 oz minced (ground) beef
10 chicken livers
50 g / 2 oz salami
5-6 ripe tomatoes
100 g / 4 oz / $^1/_2$ cup shelled peas
1 aubergine (eggplant)
2 hard-boiled eggs
1 mozzarella, grated caciocavallo (or smoked cheese)
1 onion, 1 clove of garlic, basil
Olive oil

| | |
|---|---|
| Servings: | 6 |
| Preparation time: | 30'+1 h |
| Cooking time: | 1 h 10' |
| Difficulty: | ● ● ● |
| Flavour: | ● ● ● |
| Kcal (per serving): | 826 |
| Proteins (per serving): | 44 |
| Fats (per serving): | 32 |
| Nutritional value: | ● ● ● |

1 Slice the aubergine, sprinkle with salt and leave under a weight for 30' until the bitter juices run out. Rinse and brown in 4-5 tablespoons of oil.

2 Soften the sliced onion and crushed garlic in 4-5 tablespoons of hot oil and then brown the meat and livers. Add the peas. Season with salt and pepper. Toss in the roughly-chopped tomatoes and reduce over gentle heat for half-an-hour.

3 When the pasta is cooked, drain it very much *al dente* and dress with the sauce (removing the garlic first), strips of mozzarella and the grated cheese, the sliced hard-boiled eggs, the crumbled salami and a few basil leaves. Arrange the aubergine in an oven dish and cover with an even layer of pasta, levelling it off. Bake in the oven at 180 °C / 350°F / Gas Mark 4 for 15 minutes.

# PASTICCIU DI SUSTANZA

## Pasta Crust

1 boiling fowl, 1.2 kg / 2 lb
   10 oz
1 onion
4-5 ripe tomatoes
10 chicken livers
10 veal sweetbreads
1 sausage, cinnamon
2 hard-boiled eggs and 1 yolk
Olive oil

*For the pastry:*
300 g / 11 oz / 2 cups plain
   flour
150 g / 5 oz / $^3/_4$ cup butter

| | |
|---|---|
| Servings: 6 | |
| Preparation time: 1 h + 1 h | |
| Cooking time: 1 h | |
| Difficulty: ● ● ● | |
| Flavour: ● ● ● | |
| Kcal (per serving): 1293 | |
| Proteins (per serving): 46 | |
| Fats (per serving): 61 | |
| Nutritional value: ● ● ● | |

1 Mix the softened butter into the flour and a pinch of salt. Roll out the dough, fold it over into a bar and leave to rest for 30 minutes. Roll it out again and fold over as before. Leave to rest another 30 minutes.

2 Soften the sliced onion in 4-5 table-spoons of oil in a saucepan, then, in the same pan, sauté the chicken (singed, washed and jointed) and the blanched sweetbreads. After 10 minutes, add the roughly-chopped tomatoes and the trimmed chicken livers. Cook a further 10 minutes.

3 Bone the chicken, chop up the livers and place it all in a saucepan with the sweetbreads. Add the crumbled sausage and a pinch of cinnamon and sauté over fierce heat (10 minutes).

4 Roll the dough into 2 rounds of different sizes. Use the bigger one to line a greased oven dish and spoon the stuffing over. Cover with egg slices and seal with the second circle of dough. Prick with a fork and place in the oven at 180 °C / 350 °F / Gas Mark 4 for 30'. Shortly before the end, brush the surface with egg yolk diluted in a little water.

# PASTA TUTTU PIPI

Pasta with Sweet Peppers

350 g / ¾ lb fluted sedani
  (pasta tubes)
4-5 ripe tomatoes
2 sweet peppers
1 clove of garlic
Fresh parsley
Hot red pepper
Grated pecorino cheese
Olive oil

| | |
|---|---|
| Servings: 4 | |
| Preparation time: 20' | |
| Cooking time: 30' | |
| Difficulty: ●● | |
| Flavour: ●●● | |
| Kcal (per serving): 506 | |
| Proteins (per serving): 16 | |
| Fats (per serving): 17 | |
| Nutritional value: ●● | |

Wash the sweet peppers, discarding the pith and seeds. Divide into fillets. Grill one and a half, leaving the rest raw for garnishing. Rinse, seed and dice the tomatoes.

Colour the crushed garlic in 3-4 tablespoons of oil in a frying pan, together with a sprig of parsley, the tomatoes and half the hot red pepper, crushed. Throw in the grilled peppers, roughly chopped and leave the sauce to reduce slowly (15 minutes).

Boil the pasta, drain while still firm to the bite and sauté briefly in the pepper sauce in the frying pan. Dust generously with grated pecorino and garnish with pieces of the raw pepper.

# SPAGHETTI CHI CROCCHIULI

Spaghettini with Shellfish

Scrub and beard the shellfish and get them to open in a frying pan barely covered with oil. Shell them, except for a few to use as a garnish. Sauté some chopped garlic and parsley in 4 tablespoons of oil in the frying pan and add the hot red pepper and the molluscs. Season with salt and pepper.

When the pasta is cooked, drain it nicely *al dente* and sauté briefly in the pan with the sauce. Serve, garnishing each plate with the shellfish kept aside.

| | |
|---|---|
| 350 g / $^3/_4$ lb spaghettini | |
| 300 g / 11 oz baby clams or cockles | |
| 300 g / 11 oz mussels | |
| 1 clove of garlic | |
| Fresh parsley | |
| Hot red pepper | |
| Olive oil | |

| | |
|---|---|
| **Servings:** | 4 |
| **Preparation time:** | 20' |
| **Cooking time:** | 15' |
| **Difficulty:** | ●● |
| **Flavour:** | ●● |
| **Kcal (per serving):** | 487 |
| **Proteins (per serving):** | 21 |
| **Fats (per serving):** | 13 |
| **Nutritional value:** | ●● |

# SPAGHETTI CHI MILINCIANI

Spaghetti with Aubergines (Eggplant)

350 g / ³/₄ lb spaghetti
2 small (or 1 large) aubergines (eggplant)
4-5 ripe tomatoes
1 onion
Fresh basil
Grated Parmesan cheese
Olive oil

| | |
|---|---|
| Servings: 4 | |
| Preparation time: 25'+30' | |
| Cooking time: 50' | |
| Difficulty: ● ● | |
| Flavour: ● ● | |
| Kcal (per serving): 497 | |
| Proteins (per serving): 16 | |
| Fats (per serving): 14 | |
| Nutritional value: ● ● | |

Slice the aubergines. Sprinkle with coarse salt and leave under a weight for about half-an-hour until the bitter juices run out. Rinse, dice and brown in 4 tablespoons of oil. Soften the sliced onion in 4-5 tablespoons of oil in a frying pan. Add the diced tomatoes and a sprig of basil. Season with salt and pepper. Simmer for 30 minutes, then blend the sauce in an electric blender. Boil the spaghetti and drain very much *al dente*. Dress with the tomato sauce and sauté briefly in the frying pan with the aubergine, dusting with Parmesan. Serve garnished with basil leaves.

| |
|---|
| 300 g / 11 oz / 1¹/₂ cups Italian rice |
| 200 g / 7 oz baby squid |
| 400 g / 14 oz mussels |
| 120 g / 4 oz shrimps |
| 1 anchovy |
| 3-4 ripe tomatoes |
| 1 clove of garlic |
| Fresh parsley |
| Olive oil |

| | |
|---|---|
| Servings: | 4 |
| Preparation time: | 20' |
| Cooking time: | 40' |
| Difficulty: | ● ● |
| Flavour: | ● ● |
| Kcal (per serving): | 488 |
| Proteins (per serving): | 23 |
| Fats (per serving): | 13 |
| Nutritional value: | ● ● |

# RISOTTU ACI TREZZA

Aci Trezza Risotto

Clean the mussels and get them to open in a frying pan barely covered with oil. Shell them and reserve the liquor that they have given off.
Chop the garlic and parsley up together and brown in 4 tablespoons of oil in the frying pan. Throw in the baby squid and the shrimps, trimmed and cut into pieces, and the filleted anchovy. Add the roughly-chopped tomatoes after 4-5 minutes, together with 2 tablespoons of the filtered mussel liquor. Simmer for 15 minutes, throw in the rice and continue cooking, occasionally thinning the sauce with the warm mussel liquor. Just 5 minutes before the end, add the shelled mussels. Serve immediately.

# TUMMÀLA

## Rice Timbale

400 g / 14 oz / 1³/₄ cups
   Italian vialone rice
80 g / 3 oz pork rind (optional)
1 sausage
100 g / 4 oz Sicilian toma
   cheese (or any semi-fat cow's
   cheese)
100 g / 4 oz fresh provola
   (a semi-hard cheese made
   from buffalo milk)
1 onion
Tomato purée
Fresh parsley
Dried bread crumbs
Lard (or butter)
Olive oil

*For the broth:*
1 bowling fowl, 1 kg / 2¹/₄ lb
1 carrot, 1 onion, 1 stalk
   of celery
2-3 cherry tomatoes

*For the meatballs:*
180 g / 6 oz minced (ground)
   beef
Seasoned peppered pecorino
   cheese, grated
2 eggs
1 clove of garlic
Fresh parsley
Fresh breadcrumb (one slice)
   moistened in milk

| | |
|---|---|
| Servings: 6 | |
| Preparation time: 25'+1 h | |
| Cooking time: 50' | |
| Difficulty: ●●● | |
| Flavour: ●● | |
| Kcal (per serving): 1455 | |
| Proteins (per serving): 55 | |
| Fats (per serving): 83 | |
| Nutritional value: ●●● | |

1 Mix a handful of pecorino with the minced meat, the eggs, chopped garlic and parsley, the breadcrumb (squeezed of excess moisture) and salt and pepper. Shape into meat balls. Boil the fowl with the carrot, onion, celery, tomatoes and half the meat balls.

2 Soften the second onion, sliced, in a nut of lard in a frying pan. Brown the sausage and the pork rind broken up. Add some chopped parsley, a tablespoon of tomato purée (paste) diluted in water, and the remaining meat balls. Put on the lid and simmer for 25 minutes.

*Aeolian Islands: a view over Filicudi.*

**3** Bone the fowl, chop up the flesh and keep hot with the boiled meat balls. Cook the rice in the broth, drain while *al dente* and transfer to a bowl with lots of pecorino.

**4** Line a greased oven dish with dried bread crumbs. Layer some rice in it, then the chicken, some boiled meat balls and slices of toma cheese. Make another layer of meat balls in their sauce, sausage, pork rind and diced provola cheese. Cover with the rice mixed with the remaining chicken flesh, dusting with pecorino, salt and pepper. Bake in the oven at 200 °C / 400°F / Gas Mark 6 for 10 minutes.

# RISU CHI MILINCIANI

Aubergine (Eggplant) Rice

350 g / ³/₄ lb / 1¹/₂ cups
  Italian rice
2-3 aubergines (eggplant)
4-5 ripe tomatoes
1 onion
Fresh basil, parsley, saffron
Seasoned peppered pecorino
  cheese, grated
Olive oil

| | |
|---|---|
| Servings: 6 | |
| Preparation time: 20'+1 h | |
| Cooking time: 40' | |
| Difficulty: ● ● | |
| Flavour: ● ● ● | |
| Kcal (per serving): 585 | |
| Proteins (per serving): 24 | |
| Fats (per serving): 18 | |
| Nutritional value: ● ● | |

Slice the aubergines, sprinkle with salt and leave under a weight until the bitter juices run out. After half-an-hour, rinse the vegetable and brown in 3-4 tablespoons of oil in a frying pan. Soften the sliced onion, together with lots of chopped basil and parsley, in 4-5 tablespoons of oil in the frying pan. Add the tomatoes, broken up. Season with salt and pepper and let the flavours blend gently for 15 minutes.

Boil the rice to the *al dente* stage in lightly-salted water with half a sachet of saffron powder. Drain and place a layer in a greased oven dish. Cover with the tomato and aubergine sauce. Repeat the operation until the ingredients have all been used up. Dust the top layer with cheese and bake in the oven at 200 °C / 400°F / Gas Mark 6 for 10 minutes. Serve the rice strewn with chopped basil and parsley.

# FISH AND SHELLFISH

3

# AMMIRU A' RUSSA

Scampi in a Red Sauce

700-800 g / 1 ½ - 1 ¾ lb
  scampi
2 cloves of garlic
200 g / 7oz / 1 scant cup
  freshly-made tomato sauce
Parsley
Dry white wine
Olive oil

| | |
|---|---|
| Servings: 4 | |
| Preparation time: 10' | |
| Cooking time: 10' | |
| Difficulty: ● | |
| Flavour: ●● | |
| Kcal (per serving): 324 | |
| Proteins (per serving): 30 | |
| Fats (per serving): 14 | |
| Nutritional value: ● | |

Colour the garlic in 4-5 tablespoons of oil in a frying pan, add the trimmed scampi and sauté for 3 minutes. Pour in a glass (half-cup) of wine and the tomato sauce and continue the cooking for another 5 minutes, seasoning with salt and pepper. Serve the tasty prawns immediately, after dusting them with chopped parsley.

# ARATA AMMARSALATA

Gilthead with Marsala

1 Soften the sliced onion with a pinch of ground hot red pepper in 4-5 tablespoons of oil in a frying pan. Add the peeled, diced potatoes with the needles from a twig of rosemary.

2 Clean and trim the fish. Roll in flour and fry briefly in 5 tablespoons of oil in the frying pan. Turn and pour over a glass (half cup) of Marsala and the juice from half a lemon. Transfer the fish to an oven dish, add the onion and potato sauce and bake in the oven at 180 °C/ 350°F/ Gas Mark 4 for 15 minutes, basting the fish with the juices in the dish.

1 gilthead, 1 kg / 2 ¹/₄ lb
2 potatoes
2 shallots
Half a lemon
Hot red pepper, rosemary
Plain flour
Dry Marsala
Olive oil

| | |
|---|---|
| Servings: 4 | |
| Preparation time: 20' | |
| Cooking time: 30' | |
| Difficulty: ● ● | |
| Flavour: ● ● | |
| Kcal (per serving): 441 | |
| Proteins (per serving): 37 | |
| Fats (per serving): 12 | |
| Nutritional value: ● | |

# CALAMARI CHINI

## Stuffed Squid

6 squid, 700-800 g /
1 1/2-1 1/4 lb
Dried bread crumbs
1 clove of garlic
Parsley
100 g / 4 oz Sicilian toma
cheese (or any semi-fat
cow's cheese)
Oregano
Olive oil

| | |
|---|---|
| **Servings:** 4 | |
| **Preparation time:** 25' | |
| **Cooking time:** 45' | |
| **Difficulty:** ● ● | |
| **Flavour:** ● ● | |
| **Kcal (per serving):** 382 | |
| **Proteins (per serving):** 33 | |
| **Fats (per serving):** 21 | |
| **Nutritional value:** ● | |

**2** Draw off the heat. Add the garlic and parsley, chopped up together, and stir. Season with salt and pepper.

**1** Clean the squid. Chop up the heads and tentacles, discarding the eyes, and sauté in a frying pan where you have cooked 2 good handfuls of dried bread crumbs in a trickle of olive oil.

**3** Add pieces of the cheese. Stuff the squid with the well-mixed filling and secure with a wooden toothpick. Arrange the pieces in a greased oven dish and bake in the oven at 180 °C / 350°F / Gas Mark 4 for a half-hour, brushing them with a twig of oregano dipped in oil which has been seasoned with salt and pepper.

# CALAMARICCHI E SICCI 'N TIANU

## Stewed Shellfish

C lean the shellfish, removing any cartilage, the eyes and the ink-sacs (reserving a couple of the latter). Cut the fish up into fair-sized pieces. In 4-5 tablespoons of oil in a saucepan, soften the garlic, chopped up together with the parsley, adding the filleted anchovies and a half-glass (quarter-cup) of wine. Allow the latter to evaporate over fierce heat, then lower the heat and add the diced tomatoes, half a broken-up hot red pepper and a little salt.
Cover the pan and stew gently for half-an-hour, if necessary adding a little water. Towards the end of cooking, throw in the reserved ink sacs. Stir and bring to the dinner table.

1 kg / 2 ¹/₄ lb baby squid
  and cuttlefish
4-5 ripe tomatoes
2 anchovies
1 clove of garlic
Hot red pepper, parsley
Dry white wine
Olive oil

| | |
|---|---|
| Servings: 4 | |
| Preparation time: 30' | |
| Cooking time: 40' | |
| Difficulty: ● ● | |
| Flavour: ● ● ● | |
| Kcal (per serving): 331 | |
| Proteins (per serving): 30 | |
| Fats (per serving): 14 | |
| Nutritional value: ● | |

# DENTICI O' FURNU

Baked Sea Bream

1 sea bream (1.3 kg / 2³/₄ lb)
1 onion
4 potatoes
Salted capers
Green olives
Hot red pepper, rosemary, thyme
Pre-prepared meat stock
Olive oil

| | |
|---|---|
| Servings: | 4 |
| Preparation time: | 20' |
| Cooking time: | 45' |
| Difficulty: | ● ● |
| Flavour: | ● ● |
| Kcal (per serving): | 499 |
| Proteins (per serving): | 41 |
| Fats (per serving): | 23 |
| Nutritional value: | ● ● |

Clean the sea bream and stuff the ventral cavity with a sprig of thyme, some rosemary needles, half a chopped onion and a pinch of salt. Chop up the remaining onion and soften with the peeled, diced potatoes, half a hot red pepper, a handful of olives (stoned) and capers (rinsed) in 3-4 tablespoons of oil in a frying pan. Transfer the sauce to an oven dish, arrange the sea bream on top and douse with 2-3 ladlefuls (8-12 tablespoons) of stock. Place the dish in a pre-heated oven at 180-190 °C / 350-375°F / Gas Mark 4-5 and bake for about half-an-hour, basting from time to time with more of the meat stock.

76

# LUVARU 'MPANATU

## Red Bream in a Pastry Crust

**1** Make a dough with the flour, some water in which the yeast has been dissolved, a few drops of oil and half a teaspoon of anchovy paste. Roll into a ball and leave about an hour to rest. Meanwhile, clean the red bream and parboil briefly in boiling water. Scale the fish and dress with oil, salt, pepper and a sprinkling of oregano.

**2** Roll out the pastry and lay the fish on it, together with pieces of the tomatoes. Seal the "package", following the shape of the fish, and decorate as you please. Brush with beaten egg mixed with fennel seeds. Transfer to a greased oven dish and bake in a pre-heated oven at 200 °C / 400°F / Gas Mark 6 for 40 minutes, then serve.

350 g / 12 oz / 2$^1$/$_3$ cups plain flour
15 g / 0.6 oz fresh brewer's yeast
1 red bream, 1.2 kg / 2 lb 10 oz
Anchovy paste
3-4 ripe tomatoes
1 egg yolk, beaten
Oregano, fennel seeds
Olive oil

| | |
|---|---|
| Servings: | 4 |
| Preparation time: | 30'+1 h |
| Cooking time: | 50' |
| Difficulty: | ● ● |
| Flavour: | ● ● |
| Kcal (per serving): | 739 |
| Proteins (per serving): | 52 |
| Fats (per serving): | 25 |
| Nutritional value: | ● ● |

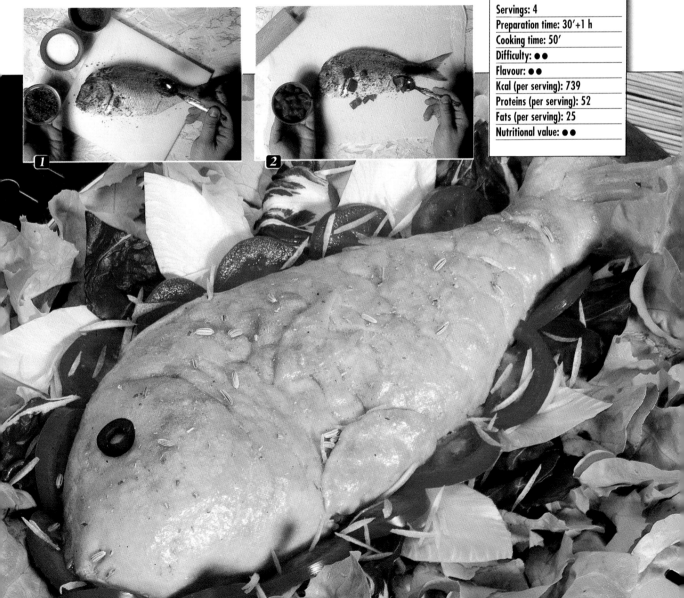

# MULETTU ALL'ACQUA DI MARI

Grey Mullet Cooked in Sea Water

1 grey mullet or 2 smaller ones,
  about 1 kg / 2 ¼ lb
4-5 potatoes
1 lemon
Parsley
Olive oil

| | |
|---|---|
| Servings: 4 | |
| Preparation time: 20′ | |
| Cooking time: 20′ | |
| Difficulty: ● | |
| Flavour: ● ● | |
| Kcal (per serving): 492 | |
| Proteins (per serving): 39 | |
| Fats (per serving): 24 | |
| Nutritional value: ● | |

Peel and boil the potatoes. Cut into small chunks. Clean the grey mullet (it should come from clean waters!) and poach in sea water in a fish kettle. If sea water is not available and the fish is fresh, water to which salt has been added is acceptable, provided that it is clear and there is no chlorine. Meanwhile, prepare the sauce. Mix 8-10 tablespoons of oil with a nice sprig of parsley, chopped up, the juice of a lemon, salt and pepper. Drain the fish, lay on a serving dish, surround it with the chunks of potato and serve with the sauce.

# PISCISPATA A' MISSINISA

Messina-Style Sword Fish

| 4 sword fish steaks, 1 kg / 2 ¼ lb |
| 1 onion |
| 4-5 ripe tomatoes |
| 3 potatoes |
| Salted capers |
| Pickled green olives |
| Parsley |
| Olive oil |

| | |
|---|---|
| Servings: | 4 |
| Preparation time: | 20' |
| Cooking time: | 40' |
| Difficulty: | ● ● |
| Flavour: | ● ● |
| Kcal (per serving): | 528 |
| Proteins (per serving): | 50 |
| Fats (per serving): | 22 |
| Nutritional value: | ● |

Soften the sliced onion in 4-5 tablespoons of oil in a frying pan, along with a dozen stoned olives, the broken-up tomatoes, a tablespoon of rinsed capers and a pinch of salt and pepper. Cover and simmer for a quarter-hour. Boil and peel the potatoes and slice. Lay the sword fish steaks with their sauce in a large pan. Add the potatoes with a sprig of parsley. Leave 10-15 minutes over gentle heat, seasoning with salt and pepper. Serve the hot fish immediately, masked in the sauce.

# PISCISPATA A LA STIMPIRATA

Sword Fish in Vinegar

4 sword fish steaks,
  1 kg / 2¹/₄ lb
2 ripe tomatoes
1 onion
1 stalk of celery
Salted capers
Pickled green olives
Flour
Vinegar
Olive oil

| | |
|---|---|
| Servings: | 4 |
| Preparation time: | 15′ |
| Cooking time: | 30′ |
| Difficulty: | ●● |
| Flavour: | ●● |
| Kcal (per serving): | 440 |
| Proteins (per serving): | 48 |
| Fats (per serving): | 22 |
| Nutritional value: | ● |

Coat the fish steaks in flour and brown on both sides in 3-4 tablespoons of oil in a frying pan. Drain and keep warm.
Along with the chopped celery, soften the sliced onion in 4-5 tablespoons of oil in a pan. Add a tablespoon of rinsed capers, a liberal handful of stoned olives, the tomatoes in small chunks, and season with salt and pepper. Pour in 4 scant tablespoons of hot water and let the flavours blend over fierce heat. When the sauce has thickened, add the fish, douse with half a glass (a quarter-cup) of vinegar and put the lid on the pan. Allow the vinegar to evaporate slowly and serve at once.

*80*

# PISCISPATA ARRUSTUTU

Grilled Sword Fish

Grill the lightly-oiled and salted fish (3-4 minutes each side) over red-hot charcoal. An electric grill may also be used. Serve immediately at the dinner table, together with the warm *sammurigghiu* sauce, prepared as laid out on page 30, with garlic, oil, oregano, parsley, lemon juice, salt and pepper. Sicilians consider this simple recipe – provided the fish is very fresh – to be the tastiest of all.

4 sword fish steaks, 1 kg / 2 1/4 lb

*"Sammurigghiu" sauce (see page 30)*

| | |
|---|---|
| **Servings:** 4 | |
| **Preparation time:** 15' | |
| **Cooking time:** 40' | |
| **Difficulty:** ● ● | |
| **Flavour:** ● ● | |
| **Kcal (per serving):** 435 | |
| **Proteins (per serving):** 46 | |
| **Fats (per serving):** 26 | |
| **Nutritional value:** ● | |

# PISCISTOCCU AGGHIOTTA

## Stockfish Delicacy

3 After 4-5 minutes, cover the fish with hot water in which a tablespoon of tomato purée (concentrate) has been dissolved. Season with salt and pepper. Add a tablespoon of pine nuts and a handful of sultanas, soaked and then squeezed dry.

4 Simmer for a good hour. Add a tablespoon of capers, the stoned olives and the chopped celery leaves. Cook another 20 minutes and serve after trickling a little oil over.

1 Soften the sliced onion in 4-5 tablespoons of oil in a pan. Add the blanched chopped celery (reserving the leaves), the finely-chopped carrot and the diced potato.

2 Add the roughly-chopped tomato and, 2-3 minutes later, the stockfish, which has been cut into chunks and coated with flour.

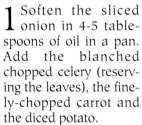

| 700 g / 1 ¹/₂ lb stockfish, soaked | 1 potato | Servings: 4 |
| 4-5 ripe tomatoes | Tomato purée (concentrate) | Preparation time: 20' |
| 100 g / 4 oz pickled green olives | Pine nuts | Cooking time: 1 h 45' |
| Salted capers | Sultanas | Difficulty: ● ● |
| ¹/₂ stalk of celery | Flour | Flavour: ● ● ● |
|   (with its leaves) | Olive oil | Kcal (per serving): 631 |
| ¹/₂ carrot | | Proteins (per serving): 45 |
| 1 onion | | Fats (per serving): 31 |
| | | Nutritional value: ● ● |

# PISCISTOCCU CHI MILINCIANI

Stock Fish with Aubergine (Eggplant)

700 g / 1 ½ lb stockfish,
  soaked
2 aubergines (eggplant)
2-3 ripe tomatoes
1 onion
1 clove of garlic
Parsley
Pickled green olives
Flour
Olive oil

| | |
|---|---|
| Servings: 4 | |
| Preparation time: 20′ | |
| Cooking time: 40′ | |
| Difficulty: ● ● | |
| Flavour: ● ●● | |
| Kcal (per serving): 376 | |
| Proteins (per serving): 38 | |
| Fats (per serving): 17 | |
| Nutritional value:● | |

C lean and slice the aubergines (eggplant) and lay for an hour on a tray, covered with coarse salt, under a weight, until the bitter liquor runs out. Rinse and dice. Coat with flour and brown in 3-4 tablespoons of boiling oil in a frying pan. Cut the stockfish into bite-sized pieces, roll in flour and brown in 4 tablespoons of oil in a separate frying pan.

Soften the sliced onion and crushed garlic in 4-5 tablespoons of oil in a pan. Add a chopped sprig of parsley with the roughly-chopped tomatoes, and reduce the sauce over fierce heat. Season with salt and pepper. Add the stockfish with the aubergines and a handful of stoned olives. Let the flavours blend slowly for 3-4 minutes, stirring continually, then serve.

# PURPICEDDU MURATU

Stewed Octopus

1 octopus, 1 kg / 2 1/4 lb
4-5 ripe tomatoes
1/2 onion
1 clove of garlic
Parsley, hot red pepper
Black cuttlefish ink (if desired)
Red wine
Olive oil

| | |
|---|---|
| Servings: 4 | |
| Preparation time: 20' | |
| Cooking time: 50' | |
| Difficulty: ●● | |
| Flavour: ●●● | |
| Kcal (per serving): 375 | |
| Proteins (per serving): 29 | |
| Fats (per serving): 18 | |
| Nutritional value: ● | |

Clean the octopus. Sauté the parsley, onion and garlic (all chopped up together) in 3-4 tablespoons of oil in a saucepan. Add the roughly-chopped tomatoes, a pinch of salt and a hot red pepper. Douse with half a glass (a quarter-cup) of red wine. Cover the container with its lid and simmer for 45 minutes. Towards the end, add a quarter of a teaspoon of black cuttlefish ink, if desired. Make sure that only after it has been left to cool slightly in its sauce is the octopus served at the dinner table. In this way, it will be tasty and tender.

*Why "muratu" or "walled up"? Well, tradition has it that the octopus was cooked in a hermetically-sealed urn-like pot. As such as container is not easily available at every latitude, we shall resort to either an earthenware casserole with a tight-fitting lid (even tied on with string) and a wire gauze beneath to spread the flame evenly, or a commonplace pressure cooker (in which case, cooking time needs to be halved).*

# SARDI A CHIAPPA

## Sardines au Gratin

1 kg / 2 ¹/₄ lb fresh sardines
(or sprats)
4 salted anchovies
Bay leaves
Nutmeg
Parsley
1 lemon
Dried bread crumbs
Olive oil

| | |
|---|---|
| Servings: 4 | |
| Preparation time: 30′ | |
| Cooking time: 35′ | |
| Difficulty: ● ● | |
| Flavour: ● ● ● | |
| Kcal (per serving): 461 | |
| Proteins (per serving): 38 | |
| Fats (per serving): 27 | |
| Nutritional value: ● | |

Clean and rinse the sardines, discarding the heads and bones. Open them out flat. Prepare the stuffing by sautéing a couple of generous handfuls of dried bread crumbs in a frying pan, turning them over with a wooden spoon. Immediately they start to colour, pour in 5-6 tablespoons of oil, stirring all the while, and fry them over fierce heat. Transfer the bread crumbs to a bowl and mix in the broken-up anchovies (trimmed of all little bones), a sprig of parsley (chopped), salt, pepper and a pinch of grated nutmeg. Stuff the sardines with the mixture and arrange them in a greased oven dish, separating each with a bay leaf. Sprinkle over the bread crumbs, drizzle with oil and place in a pre-heated oven at 180 °C / 350°F / Gas Mark 4. After half-an-hour, remove from the oven, sprinkle with lemon juice and serve immediately.

# SPINULA 'NCARTATA

## Foil-Wrapped Bass

Clean the bass and lay on an oiled sheet of foil, together with the diced tomatoes, a handful of oregano, a spoonful of rinsed capers, salt and pepper. Fold the foil over and seal the edges of the "package". Arrange in a greased oven dish and place in a pre-heated oven for 30 minutes at 180 °C / 350°F / Gas Mark 4. Take out of the oven and serve.

1.2 kg / 2 lb 10 oz bass
5-6 ripe tomatoes
Salted capers
Oregano
Olive oil

| | |
|---|---|
| Servings: 4 | |
| Preparation time: 15' | |
| Cooking time: 30' | |
| Difficulty: ● ● | |
| Flavour: ● ● | |
| Kcal (per serving): 378 | |
| Proteins (per serving): 33 | |
| Fats (per serving): 22 | |
| Nutritional value: ● | |

# SARDI A BECCAFICU

Stuffed Sardines

1 kg / 2 ¼ lb fresh sardines
   (or sprats)
4 salted anchovies
1 lemon
Dried bread crumbs
Pine nuts
Sultanas
Bay leaves, parsley
Granulated sugar
Olive oil

| | |
|---|---|
| Servings: 4 | |
| Preparation time: 30′ | |
| Cooking time: 35′ | |
| Difficulty: ● ● | |
| Flavour: ● ● ● | |
| Kcal (per serving): 668 | |
| Proteins (per serving): 46 | |
| Fats (per serving): 34 | |
| Nutritional value: ● ● | |

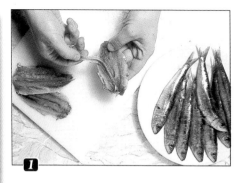

**1** Rinse the sardines under running water and trim them, discarding the heads and bones. Open them out flat and allow to drain, one on top of the other.

**2** Toast a couple of generous handfuls of dried bread crumbs in 3-4 tablespoons of oil in a frying pan. In a bowl, mix with the anchovies, broken up and cleaned of all little bones, a sprig of parsley (chopped), a handful of soaked sultanas (squeezed of excess moisture), a handful of pine nuts, salt and pepper.

**3** Stuff the sardines with the mixture and close them up. Lay them in a greased oven dish, each one separated by a bay leaf. Sprinkle over the bread crumbs, dress with a little oil and the lemon juice in which a teaspoon of sugar has been dissolved. Bake in a pre-heated oven at 180 °C / 350°F / Gas Mark 4 for half-an-hour. Take out and serve.

# TRIGGHI 'N TIANU

## Red Mullet (Surmullet) in Tomato Sauce

1 kg / 2$^1$/$_4$ lb striped red
 mullet (surmullet)
4-5 ripe tomatoes
2 cloves of garlic
Oregano, parsley
Olive oil

| | |
|---|---|
| Servings: 4 | |
| Preparation time: 20' | |
| Cooking time: 20' | |
| Difficulty: ●● | |
| Flavour: ●● | |
| Kcal (per serving): 359 | |
| Proteins (per serving): 43 | |
| Fats (per serving): 16 | |
| Nutritional value: ● | |

Wash and trim the mullet. Sauté a clove of garlic in 3-4 table-spoons of oil in a frying pan. Take out the garlic, then simmer the pieces of tomato in the oil. Add the other garlic, chopped up, with salt and pepper. Allow the sauce to reduce for about ten minutes, then add the mullet, letting it absorb the flavours for 6-7 minutes on each side. Check the seasoning of salt and pepper. Before serving, dust with oregano.

# TUNNINA CA CIPUDDATA

Tuna fish, Onion and Vinegar

Coat the tuna fish steaks with flour. Brown in 4-5 tablespoons of oil in a frying pan. Drain and keep warm. Soften the sliced onion in 4-5 tablespoons of oil in a saucepan. Souse with a scant glass (scant half-cup) of vinegar, then add the fish. Allow the flavours to be absorbed briefly. Add a sprig of parsley, chopped up and stir. Check the seasoning of salt and pepper, sprinkle a little vinegar over and serve. A tasty dish which can be eaten either hot or cold.

4 tuna fish steaks
  (800 g / 1 ³/₄ lb)
1 onion
Parsley
Flour
White wine vinegar
Olive oil

| | |
|---|---|
| Servings: | 4 |
| Preparation time: | 10' |
| Cooking time: | 20' |
| Difficulty: | ● ● |
| Flavour: | ● ● |
| Kcal (per serving): | 459 |
| Proteins (per serving): | 45 |
| Fats (per serving): | 21 |
| Nutritional value: | ● |

# TUNNU A LA MATALOTTA

Tuna Fish in Pickle Sauce

4 steaks tuna saucepan fish
(800 g / 1³/₄ lb)
4-5 ripe tomatoes
Dried bread crumbs
Salted capers
Pickled green olives
Mint, parsley
Olive oil

| | |
|---|---|
| Servings: | 4 |
| Preparation time: | 15' |
| Cooking time: | 30' |
| Difficulty: | ●● |
| Flavour: | ●●● |
| Kcal (per serving): | 448 |
| Proteins (per serving): | 45 |
| Fats (per serving): | 21 |
| Nutritional value: | ●● |

1 Place the tuna steaks in a dish. Add a tablespoon of rinsed capers, a scant handful of stoned olives, the diced tomato, salt and pepper. Pour in enough water to almost cover the ingredients.

2 Cook over fierce heat until the water in the pan has largely evaporated. Dredge with dried bread crumbs, the mint and parsley all chopped up together and seasoned with a little oil, salt and pepper. Transfer to an oven dish and bake for about 10 minutes. Serve the steaks well-masked in their sauce.

# MEAT

4

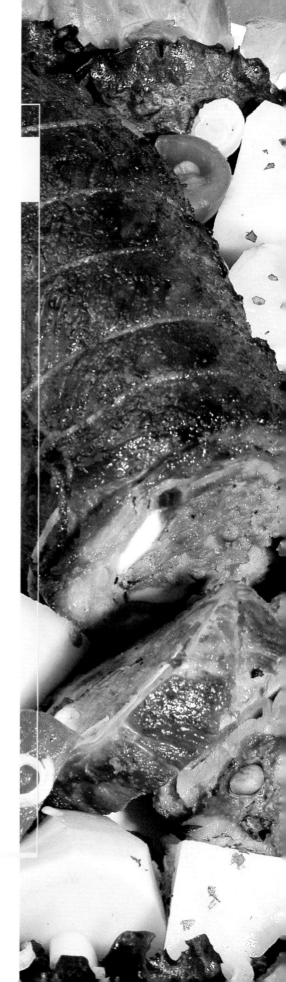

# AGNEDDU AGGLASSATU

## Lamb Casserole

**1** Soften the sliced onion in a saucepan with 4-5 tablespoons of oil. As soon as it begins to colour, add a nut of lard, the chopped garlic, a sprig of parsley (chopped) and the lamb.

**2** Brown evenly all over, seasoning with salt and pepper. Pour in a scant cup of chicken stock.

**3** Peel the potatoes, cut into pieces, add to the lamb and cover the pan with the lid. Leave to simmer for about an hour, checking the salt and pepper.

**4** Five minutes before the end, add shaves of freshly-ripened pecorino cheese and a good handful of the grated cheese. Stir, draw off the heat and serve.

1 kg / 2¼ lb shoulder of lamb, boned and cubed
600 g / 1 lb 5 oz new potatoes
1 onion
2-3 cloves of garlic
Parsley
60 g / 7oz newly-ripened pecorino cheese

Seasoned pecorino cheese, grated
Pre-prepared chicken stock
Lard
Olive oil

Servings: 4
Preparation time: 30'
Cooking time: 1 h 20'
Difficulty: ● ●
Flavour: ● ● ●
Kcal (per serving): 675
Proteins (per serving): 50
Fats (per serving): 39
Nutritional value: ● ●

# CUNIGGHIU A' CACCIATURA

Rabbit Cacciatora

1 rabbit, approx. 1.2 kg / 2 lb
  10 oz
1 onion
1 stalk of celery
1 clove of garlic
Salted capers
Pickled green olives
Parsley
Tomato purée (concentrate)
Flour
Dry Marsala
Olive oil

| | |
|---|---|
| Servings: 4 | |
| Preparation time: 25'+2 h | |
| Cooking time: 1 h | |
| Difficulty: ●● | |
| Flavour: ●●● | |
| Kcal (per serving): 527 | |
| Proteins (per serving): 42 | |
| Fats (per serving): 23 | |
| Nutritional value: ●● | |

1 Wash and joint the rabbit and marinade in a bowl with 2 full glasses (1 cup) of Marsala for a couple of hours.

2 Colour the sliced onion with the chopped garlic and parsley in 4-5 tablespoons of oil in a frying pan. Then brown the rabbit pieces which have been drained, floured and seasoned with salt and pepper.

3 Add a scant tablespoon of tomato purée (concentrate) diluted in a cup of hot water. Simmer for half-an-hour.

4 Add a tablespoon of rinsed capers, the chopped celery and a handful of olives. Let the flavours blend slowly for another half-hour. Baste from time to time with the marinade.

# CUNIGGHIU A LA STIMPIRATA

Sweet-Sour Rabbit

| |
|---|
| 1 rabbit, approx. 1.2 kg / 2 lb 10 oz |
| 1 onion |
| 1 stalk of celery |
| Salted capers |
| Pickled green olives |
| Flour, sugar |
| Vinegar, dry white wine |
| Olive oil |

| | |
|---|---|
| Servings: | 4 |
| Preparation time: | 20' |
| Cooking time: | 1 h |
| Difficulty: | ● ● |
| Flavour: | ● ● ● |
| Kcal (per serving): | 524 |
| Proteins (per serving): | 42 |
| Fats (per serving): | 23 |
| Nutritional value: | ● ● |

Wash and joint the rabbit. Coat with flour. Brown in 4-5 tablespoons of oil in a frying pan. Pour over a scant glass (scant half-cup) of vinegar and add a teaspoon of sugar. As soon as the vinegar has evaporated, draw off the heat, cover the pan and keep warm. Soften the chopped onion and celery slowly in another pan with 4-5 tablespoons of oil. Throw in a tablespoon of rinsed capers and a handful of stoned olives which have been broken up. Season with salt and pepper. Transfer the sauce to an ovenware dish, together with the rabbit and the cooking juices in the pan. Douse with half a glass (a quarter-cup) of wine, adjust the salt and pepper and bake in a pre-heated oven at 180 °C / 350°F / Gas Mark 4 for 35-40 minutes.

# FARSUMAGRU

## Stuffed Meat Roll

500 g / 1 lb 2 oz veal
  (in 1 piece)
Home-made tomato sauce
Red wine
Olive oil, lard (optional)

*For the stuffing:*
1 sausage
140 g / 4 $^{1}/_{2}$ oz prosciutto
  rashers
60 g / 2 oz minced (ground)
  beef
70 g / 3 oz streaky bacon
1 egg, plus 2 hard-boiled eggs
1 spring onion
1 clove of garlic
80 g / 3 oz / $^{1}/_{3}$ cup shelled
  peas
80 g / 3 oz piquant
  caciocavallo or provolone
  cheese
Peppered pecorino cheese,
  grated
Parsley

| | |
|---|---|
| Servings: 4 | |
| Preparation time: 40′ | |
| Cooking time: 1 h 15′ | |
| Difficulty: ● ● ● | |
| Flavour: ● ● ● | |
| Kcal (per serving): 1069 | |
| Proteins (per serving): 64 | |
| Fats (per serving): 77 | |
| Nutritional value: ● ● ● | |

1 Beat out the veal, giving it the shape of a regular rectangle as far as possible. Cover with prosciutto rashers and rings of hard-boiled egg.

2 Arrange strips of bacon and caciocavallo (or provolone) cheese length ways down the meat. Sprinkle over some chopped chives, parsley and garlic.

3 Incorporate a beaten egg into the minced (ground) meat, along with a handful of grated pecorino cheese, the peas, the crumbled sausage, salt and pepper. Spread the mixture on the veal in an even layer.

**4** Roll up the meat strip and tie tightly with string. Brown in 3-4 tablespoons of oil and a nut of lard (if desired) in the frying pan. Pour in a glass (half cup) of wine, allow to evaporate and add the tomato sauce, diluted slightly with a little water. Put on the lid and leave to cook slowly for about an hour. When the meat is cooked, untie the string and serve the meat roll in its sauce.

# CUSTIGGHI SARTATI

## Sautéed Pork Chops

1.3 kg / 2 3/4 lb pork chops
1 large onion
Parsley

| | |
|---|---|
| **Servings:** 4 | |
| **Preparation time:** 10' | |
| **Cooking time:** 20' | |
| **Difficulty:** ● | |
| **Flavour:** ● ● | |
| **Kcal (per serving):** 258 | |
| **Proteins (per serving):** 35 | |
| **Fats (per serving):** 11 | |
| **Nutritional value:** ● | |

If the butcher has not already done so, separate the chops and sauté over fierce heat in a frying pan with the bottom barely covered in water. Turn the pieces over frequently. Season with salt and pepper and place the meat on a serving dish, keeping it hot.
Slice the onion and sauté in the pan in the pork fat. Serve the chops accompanied with the onion in rings, dust with chopped parsley and mask in the residue from the pan.

# JADDUZZU SUFFRITTU

## Stewed Chicken

Prepare the chicken for stewing and cut into pieces. Soften the sliced onion in 4-5 tablespoons of oil in a saucepan. Brown the chicken evenly all over. Season with salt and pepper and flavour with the needles from a twig of rosemary. Pour in a glass (half-cup) of wine and allow to evaporate over gentle heat.

Simmer for a quarter-hour, then add a sprig of parsley (chopped) and stir once more. Check for salt and pepper. Cook slowly for roughly a further quarter-hour (if necessary adding a little hot water) until the cooking juices thicken. Serve the chicken hot.

1 roasting chicken or poussin,
  1.2 kg / 2 lb 10 oz
Half an onion
Rosemary
Parsley
Red wine
Olive oil

| | |
|---|---|
| Servings: 4 | |
| Preparation time: 20' | |
| Cooking time: 40' | |
| Difficulty: ● ● | |
| Flavour: ● ● | |
| Kcal (per serving): 667 | |
| Proteins (per serving): 38 | |
| Fats (per serving): 48 | |
| Nutritional value: ● ● | |

# JADDUZZU ZOGGHIATU

## Chicken in a Mint Sauce

1 chicken, 1.2 kg / 2 lb 10 oz
Flour
Olive oil
"Zogghiu" sauce (see page 34),
   with mint, parsley, garlic,
   vinegar and olive oil

| | |
|---|---|
| Servings: | 4 |
| Preparation time: | 30'+30' |
| Cooking time: | 45' |
| Difficulty: | ● |
| Flavour: | ● ● |
| Kcal (per serving): | 684 |
| Proteins (per serving): | 35 |
| Fats (per serving): | 54 |
| Nutritional value: | ● ● |

Prepare the *zogghiu* sauce according to the instructions on page 34, blending a good handful of mint leaves, a sprig of parsley and a clove of garlic in an electric blender. Season the resultant smooth, thick pulp with 6 tablespoons of oil, the same quantity of vinegar, salt and pepper. Set aside to rest for half-an-hour.

When the chicken is ready for cooking, season with salt and pepper brush with a little oil and grill (broil). Otherwise, you could joint the chicken and sauté it in 4-5 tablespoons of oil in a frying pan. However you cook it, serve it steaming hot, accompanied by its delicious sauce.

# SCACCIA DI MAIALI

Pork Patty

350 g / ³/₄ lb / 2¹/₃ cups flour
15 g / 0.6 oz fresh brewer's
   yeast or 2 ¹/₄ tsp active dry
   yeast
700 g / 1¹/₂ lb minced
   (ground) pork
Grated pecorino cheese
Parsley, 1 lemon
Lard, olive oil

| | |
|---|---|
| Servings: 4 | |
| Preparation time: 25'+1 h | |
| Cooking time: 30' | |
| Difficulty: | ● ● |
| Flavour: | ● ● |
| Kcal (per serving): 816 | |
| Proteins (per serving): 47 | |
| Fats (per serving): 37 | |
| Nutritional value: | ● ● ● |

1 Dissolve the yeast in water and mix into the flour with a few drops of oil and a pinch of salt. Shape into a ball and leave an hour to rest. Mix the minced meat in a bowl with a sprig of chopped parsley, salt, pepper, the juice of a lemon and a handful of grated pecorino cheese.

2 Roll the dough out into a round, about a quarter-of-an-inch thick. Grease with lard and spoon the filling over one side. Fold the dough over the stuffing (like a Cornish patty) and seal the edges. Lightly grease the patty with lard and place in an oven dish. Bake in a pre-heated oven at 200 °C / 400°F / Gas Mark 6 for 30 minutes.

# SPITINI DI PRIMUSALI

## Cheese Skewers

250 g / 9 oz minced (ground) beef

200 g / 7 oz primosale (or unsmoked provola) cheese

2 fresh sausages

1 spring onion

2 eggs

4-5 slices white Italian bread

Dried bread crumbs

Basil

Seasoned pecorino cheese

Milk

Red wine

Oil for frying

| | |
|---|---|
| Servings: 4 | |
| Preparation time: 25'+15' | |
| Cooking time: 30' | |
| Difficulty: ● ● | |
| Flavour: ● ● | |
| Kcal (per serving): 997 | |
| Proteins (per serving): 46 | |
| Fats (per serving): 63 | |
| Nutritional value: ● ● ● | |

Soak the bread slices in the milk for a quarter-of-an-hour. In a bowl, mix the minced (ground) meat with the finely-chopped spring onion, a few leaves of basil (chopped), a generous handful of grated pecorino, a fistful of bread crumbs, salt and pepper. Incorporate a beaten egg into the mixture. Shape into little meatballs.

Sauté rounds of sausage in a frying pan with half a glass (a quarter-cup) of wine. Remove the sausage and sauté cubes of the bread (after squeezing out excess moisture) in the same pan.

Thread the skewers, alternating a meat ball, a cube of bread, a chunk of cheese and a disc of sausage, continuing until all the ingredients have been used up. Dip the skewers into a beaten egg and then in the bread crumbs, rolling them around to coat evenly. Fry in plenty of boiling oil, drain and serve at once.

# VEGETABLE, SALAD AND EGG DISHES

5

# L'NZALATA D'ARANCI

## Orange Salad

6 oranges
  (preferably not too ripe)
2-3 sprigs of parsley
Olive oil

Servings: 4
Preparation time: 15'
Difficulty: ●
Flavour: ●
Kcal (per serving): 210
Proteins (per serving): 2
Fats (per serving): 15
Nutritional value: ● ● ●

Peel the oranges and remove the white pith. Separate the segments one by one and cut to pieces, stripping them of the skin covering them. Arrange on a serving dish and sprinkle with some chopped parsley. Dress the salad with a trickle of olive oil, a little salt and a grinding of black pepper. This is a delicacy to accompany roast meat.

# 'NZALATA 'U FURNU

## Oven Salad

3-4 onions
2 ripe tomatoes
Fresh oregano
Olive oil

Servings: 4
Preparation time: 15'
Cooking time: 30'
Difficulty: ●
Flavour: ● ●
Kcal (per serving): 137
Proteins (per serving): 2
Fats (per serving): 10
Nutritional value: ● ●

Trim the onions and arrange in a greased oven dish. Place in a pre-heated oven at 180 °C / 350°F / Gas Mark 4 for half-an-hour. Take out and remove the outer layer of the onions. Slice the hearts and put them with wedges of tomato in a bowl. Dress with olive oil, salt, pepper and a handful of fresh oregano.
If you prefer something richer, add a filleted anchovy, broken up, along with 2 hard-boiled eggs cut into wedges or rings.

# CUCUZZEDDI FRITTI

Fried Courgettes (Zucchini)

Lightly toast a handful of bread crumbs in a frying pan. Clean the courgettes (zucchini), slice and fry, along with a clove of garlic, in 4-5 tablespoons of oil in the pan until golden. Make a layer in an oven dish (discarding the garlic), sprinkle with bread crumbs and a few tarragon, mint and fresh oregano leaves. Season with salt and pepper. Form a second layer of courgettes, sprinkle some bread crumbs, herbs, salt and pepper over, and repeat the operation until all the ingredients have been used up. Pour over a little oil, sprinkle in some vinegar, add a hot red pepper (broken into pieces) and place the dish in the oven at 200 °C / 400°F / Gas Mark 6 for 10 minutes. Very good when eaten straight from the oven, but they are also delicious when cooled.

4-5 courgettes (zucchini)
1 clove of garlic
Dried bread crumbs
Tarragon, mint and oregano
Hot red pepper
Vinegar
Olive oil

| | |
|---|---|
| Servings: | 4 |
| Preparation time: | 30' |
| Cooking time: | 20' |
| Difficulty: | ● ● |
| Flavour: | ● ● |
| Kcal (per serving): | 163 |
| Proteins (per serving): | 3 |
| Fats (per serving): | 10 |
| Nutritional value: | ● ● ● |

# SFURMATU DI CACOCCIULI

## Timbale of Artichoke

Trim the artichokes, discarding the tough leaves. Cut into wedges. Blanch 5-6 minutes in lightly-salted water, drain and purée in an electric blender. Soften the sliced onion with a sprig of chopped parsley in 3-4 tablespoons of oil in a frying pan and mix in with the artichoke purée in a bowl. Little by little, add a soup ladle (4 tablespoons) of stock, the beaten eggs and a pinch of salt and pepper. Turn the mixture into a greased oven dish.

Prepare the white sauce; work a level tablespoon of flour into the melted butter in a little saucepan. Add, stirring slowly over gentle heat, 2 soup ladles (8 tablespoons) of hot stock, a little at a time. Adjust the salt. When thickened, pour the sauce into the oven dish, sprinkle with Parmesan cheese and cover with a sheet of greaseproof (waxed) paper. Place the dish in a pre-heated oven at 180 °C / 350°F / Gas Mark 4 and bake for about 20 minutes.

8 globe artichokes
1 onion
Parsley
Vegetable stock
2 eggs
Grated Parmesan
Olive oil

*For the white sauce:*
Flour
Vegetable stock
30 g / 1oz / 2 tbsp butter

| | |
|---|---|
| Servings: | 4 |
| Preparation time: | 30′ |
| Cooking time: | 40′ |
| Difficulty: | ●● |
| Flavour: | ●● |
| Kcal (per serving): | 385 |
| Proteins (per serving): | 15 |
| Fats (per serving): | 25 |
| Nutritional value: | ●●● |

# OVA ALL'ACITU

## Savoury Eggs

4 eggs
Oregano
4 slices of continental bread
Vinegar
Olive oil

*For the sauce:*
1 ripe tomato
2 anchovies
1 spring onion
1 clove of garlic
Pickled green olives
Oregano, parsley
Lemon rind

Servings: 4

Preparation time: 5'

Cooking time: 5'

Difficulty: ●

Flavour: ● ●

Kcal (per serving): 390

Proteins (per serving): 15

Fats (per serving): 20

Nutritional value: ● ●

Fry the eggs in a pan with 4-5 tablespoons of oil. Season with salt and pepper, dust with oregano and sprinkle with vinegar. Put the lid on the pan and allow the eggs to absorb the seasoning a moment. Serve the eggs on toasted bread and enrich with the sauce, prepared as follows. Clean the tomato, seed, cut to pieces and purée in a blender with the rinsed and filleted anchovies, rings of onion, the garlic, a handful of stoned olives, a sprig of both oregano and parsley, and the lemon rind. Delicious.

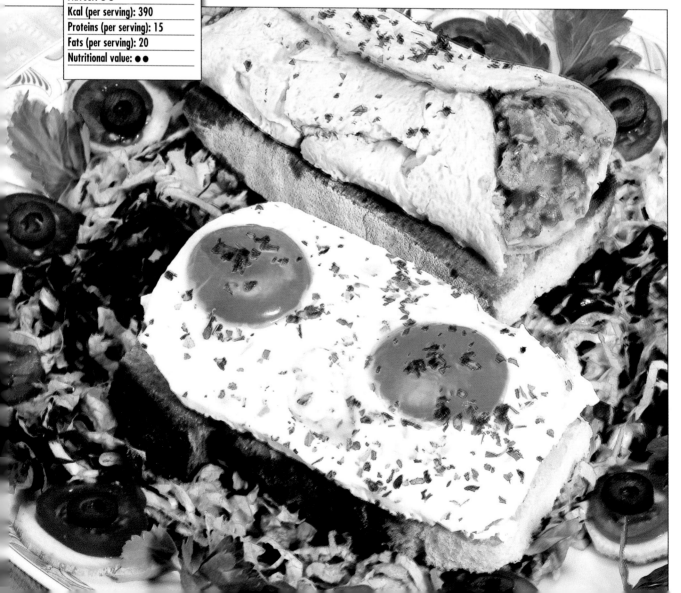

# OVA A SPIZZATINU

Soused Eggs

4 eggs
1 onion
Parsley, saffron
4 slices of continental bread
Vegetable stock
40 g / 1¹/₂ oz / 3 tbsp butter
Olive oil

| | |
|---|---|
| Servings: 4 | |
| Preparation time: 10' | |
| Cooking time: 25' | |
| Difficulty: ● ● | |
| Flavour: ● ● | |
| Kcal (per serving): 515 | |
| Proteins (per serving): 15 | |
| Fats (per serving): 33 | |
| Nutritional value: ● ● | |

Hard boil the eggs for 7 minutes. Allow to cool, then shell them. Soften the sliced onion with a sprig of parsley in 4-5 table-spoons of oil in a saucepan. Pour in a teacup of stock in which a sachet of saffron has been dissolved. Cut the hard-boiled eggs into halves and add to the pan. Cook slowly until the stock has thickened. Season with salt and pepper. Serve the *spizzatinu* with bread cubes fried in butter until golden.

# OVA DURI CA SARSA

Hard-Boiled Eggs in a Sauce

4 eggs
1 egg white
Freshly-made tomato sauce
Flour
Olive oil

| | |
|---|---|
| Servings: 4 | |
| Preparation time: 10' | |
| Cooking time: 10' | |
| Difficulty: ● | |
| Flavour: ● | |
| Kcal (per serving): 469 | |
| Proteins (per serving): 15 | |
| Fats (per serving): 37 | |
| Nutritional value: ● ● ● | |

Hard boil the eggs for 7 minutes, allow to cool, then shell them. Halve and dip in the beaten egg white. Coat with flour and fry in boiling hot oil in a frying pan. As soon as they turn golden, drain and arrange in an oven dish over a layer of tomato sauce (2-3 soup ladles or 8-12 tablespoons) in the bottom. Season with salt and pepper and place the dish in the oven at 160 °C / 300 °F / Gas Mark 2 for 10 minutes until the sauce has thickened a little. Serve at once. If you wish, you may dust the eggs with grated cheese.

# Ova Sarviati

Eggs with Sage

4 eggs
6 cloves of garlic
Salted capers
Parsley
Sage
Breadcrumb from 1 slice
  of white continental bread
Vinegar

| | |
|---|---|
| Servings: | 4 |
| Preparation time: | 20'+15' |
| Cooking time: | 17' |
| Difficulty: | ● |
| Flavour: | ● ● |
| Kcal (per serving): | 224 |
| Proteins (per serving): | 12 |
| Fats (per serving): | 10 |
| Nutritional value: | ● ● |

Soak the breadcrumb in half-an-inch of vinegar for a quarter-hour. Blanch the garlic in water without any salt for 10 minutes. Hard boil the eggs for 7 minutes, allow to cool and shell them. Chop a tablespoon of rinsed capers, a sprig of sage, the cloves of garlic and the breadcrumb (squeezed of excess moisture) in a blender. When the purée flows evenly, season with a pinch of salt and pepper. Pour the sauce onto a serving dish, lay the eggs cut into wedges on top and dredge with chopped parsley and sage.

# MILLASSATA CU BASILICÒ

Basil Omelette

4-5 eggs
Dried bread crumbs
Basil
Grated pecorino cheese
Olive oil

| | |
|---|---|
| Servings: 4 | |
| Preparation time: 10′ | |
| Cooking time: 10′ | |
| Difficulty: ● | |
| Flavour: ● | |
| Kcal (per serving): 437 | |
| Proteins (per serving): 20 | |
| Fats (per serving): 33 | |
| Nutritional value: ● ● | |

Whisk the eggs in a bowl, adding a pinch of salt and pepper, a handful of pecorino, a tablespoon of bread crumbs and the chopped leaves from a sprig of basil. Cook the omelette in a very hot frying pan (better if made of iron), with a thin layer of oil barely covering the bottom. Turn it over to set on the other side and serve immediately.

# DESSERTS AND PASTRIES

6

# BIANCUMANCIARI

## Blancmange

Pour the milk into a milkpan. Gradually stir in the sugar, a liberal tablespoon of cornflour (cornstarch) and half of the finely-grated lemon rind. Heat very gently, continuing to stir, until the sauce begins to thicken. Do not allow it to come to the boil. When it starts to come away from the sides of the pan, turn into individual bowls and leave until completely cool. Serve the *biancumanciari* at room temperature, dusting with the remaining grated lemon rind.

1 l / 1 ³/₄ pt / 4 ²/₃ cups milk
100 g / 4 oz / ¹/₂ cup
   granulated sugar
Cornflour (Cornstarch)
1 lemon

| | |
|---|---|
| **Servings:** 4 | |
| **Preparation time:** 10' | |
| **Cooking time:** 10' | |
| **Difficulty:** ● | |
| **Kcal (per serving):** 271 | |
| **Proteins (per serving):** 10 | |
| **Fats (per serving):** 8 | |
| **Nutritional value:** ● ● ● | |

# CANNOLA

Sicilian Cannoli (Ricotta Snaps)

150 g / 5 oz / 1 cup plain flour
Bitter chocolate
1 egg
Granulated sugar, salt
Marsala
40 g / 1¹/₂ oz / 3 tbsp butter
Olive oil

*For the filling:*
450 g / 1 lb / 2¹/₄ cups
   ricotta cheese
250 g / 9 oz / 2 cups icing
   (confectioner's) sugar
120 g / 5 oz plain (semi-sweet)
   chocolate
Chopped pistacchio nuts
A pinch of ground cinnamon
Candied pumpkin
   and orange peel

| | |
|---|---|
| Servings: 6 | |
| Preparation time: 25'+1 h | |
| Cooking time: 15' | |
| Difficulty: ● ● | |
| Kcal (per serving): 1221 | |
| Proteins (per serving): 17 | |
| Fats (per serving): 72 | |
| Nutritional value: ● ● ● | |

To make the *cannoli*, you will need 12 reed or steel *cannoli* cylinders. Work the flour with the egg, butter, sugar, a teaspoon of cocoa dissolved in a liqueur glass of Marsala, and a pinch of salt. When the mixture is smooth and even, allow to rest for about an hour. Roll out into a thin sheet. Cut out 4-inch squares and wrap them diagonally around the cylinders. Press the edges together delicately with a dampened finger. Heat an inch of oil in a frying pan and immerse the dough-covered pipes. Remove when they are golden and allow to cool.

With the aid of a spatula, stir 200 g (7 oz / 2 cups) icing (confectioner's) sugar, a grinding of cinnamon and a few drops of milk into the ricotta. You should obtain a fairly thick, smooth cream. Mix in the chocolate (broken into small pieces), a tablespoon of diced candied pumpkin, and a handful of shelled, blanched and chopped pistachios. With great care, slip the snaps off the cylinders and, using a teaspoon, fill them with the ricotta cream. Garnish with pieces of candied orange peel and dust with sugar.

# CASSATA

## Sicilian Cassata

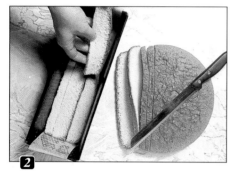

3 Pour the ricotta cream into the mould, level the top and chill the cassata in the refrigerator for a couple of hours until it sets.

4 Remove the mould from the refrigerator and turn out onto a serving dish. Decorate with the glacé icing (frosting), the diced candied fruit, strips of candied pumpkin, orange peel and sugared almonds.

1 Work the icing (confectioner's) sugar, a drop of vanilla and a liqueur glass of rum into the ricotta in a bowl. Stir in the chocolate, broken into pieces, and 2 tablespoons of diced candied fruit.

2 Line a mould with kitchen paper and cover it with slices of sponge cake. Use a little of the ricotta cream so that it sticks to the sides of the tin.

*To prepare the glacé icing (frosting), stiffly whisk 3-4 egg whites, weighing about 60 g or 2 oz, with 200 g (7 oz / 2 cups) icing (confectioner's) sugar. Add enough lemon juice to give the icing pouring consistency (it will set later) and pistachio green colouring.*

118

150 g / 5 oz sponge cake
450 g / 1 lb / 2¹/₄ cups ricotta
120 g / 5 oz / 1 cup icing
   (confectioner's) sugar
1 bar of plain (semi-sweet) chocolate
50 g / 2 oz / ¹/₄ cup candied
   orange peel
Vanilla essence

Rum
Pistachio nut glacé icing (frosting)
   (see page 118)
Candied fruit, pumpkin
   and orange peel
Silver sugared almonds
   (or any other decorations
   you like)

Servings: 4
Preparation time: 40'+2 h
Difficulty: ● ●
Kcal (per serving): 916
Proteins (per serving): 23
Fats (per serving): 24
Nutritional value: ● ● ●

# CREMA CA FRUTTA 'NCILIPPATA

Custard with Candied Fruit

200 g / 7 oz / 1 cup granulated sugar
4 egg yolks
6 dl / 1 pt / 2 ¼ cups milk
200 g / 7 oz / 1 cup candied fruit
1 lemon
Vanilla essence
Powdered cinnamon
Cornflour (cornstarch)

| | |
|---|---|
| Servings: | 4 |
| Preparation time: | 30' |
| Cooking time: | 20' |
| Difficulty: | ● ● |
| Kcal (per serving): | 576 |
| Proteins (per serving): | 17 |
| Fats (per serving): | 14 |
| Nutritional value: | ● ● ● |

Whisk the egg yolks in a bowl together with the sugar. Dilute a liberal tablespoon of cornflour with the milk in a little pan, adding a little at a time. Stirring carefully, add the beaten egg yolk, a drop of vanilla essence, the grated rind from one lemon and a quarter-teaspoon of cinnamon.
Place the pan over very gentle heat until the custard has thickened (but do not allow it to boil). Draw off the flame, turn into a dessert bowl and add the diced candied fruit.

# GATTÒ DI RICOTTA

Ricotta Gateau

S oak a handful of sultanas for twenty minutes. Slice the toma cheese and dice a full tablespoon of candied pumpkin.
With a spatula, incorporate the sugar delicately into the ricotta. Whisk the egg whites stiffly and fold into the beaten egg yolk, a little at a time, along with the ricotta mixture, a pinch of cinnamon, a drop of vanilla, the cheese, the candied pumpkin and the sultanas (after you have squeezed the water out).
Grease a cake tin with lard and coat the bottom and sides with dried bread crumbs and some finely-chopped almonds (a good handful). Spoon in the mixture, level it off and bake in a bain-marie (water bath) in the oven at 180 °C / 350°F / Gas Mark 4 for 40 minutes.

200 g / 8 oz fresh ricotta cheese
4 eggs
100 g / 4 oz / $^1/_2$ cup
  granulated sugar
80 g / 3 oz Sicilian toma
  cheese (or any semi-fat cow's
  cheese)
Ground cinnamon, shelled
  almonds, sultanas
Candied pumpkin
Dried bread crumbs
30 g / 1 oz / 2 tbsp lard
  (or butter)
Vanilla essence

| | |
|---|---|
| Servings: 4 | |
| Preparation time: 30'+20' | |
| Cooking time: 40' | |
| Difficulty: ●● | |
| Kcal (per serving): 645 | |
| Proteins (per serving): 21 | |
| Fats (per serving): 40 | |
| Nutritional value: ●●● | |

# MINNI DI VIRGINI

Candied Fruit Custard Tarts

400 g / 14 oz / 2²/₃ cups flour
150 g / 5 oz / ³/₄ cup
  granulated sugar
150 g / 5 oz / ³/₄ cup lard
Confectioner's custard
  (see below)
1 egg
Milk
Plain (semi-sweet) chocolate
  (half a bar), candied pumpkin
Icing (Confectioner's) sugar

| | |
|---|---|
| Servings: 4 | |
| Preparation time: 1 h + 1 h | |
| Cooking time: 20′ | |
| Difficulty: ● ● | |
| Kcal (per serving): 1578 | |
| Proteins (per serving): 31 | |
| Fats (per serving): 76 | |
| Nutritional value: ● ● ● | |

1 Mix the flour into the milk (about a glass or half a cup) along with the sugar and the lard, until you have a smooth, fluid dough. Form a ball and leave an hour to rest. Roll out the dough into two differently-sized sheets. At regular intervals, place spoonfuls of confectioner's custard, mixed with cubes of candied pumpkin (a tablespoon) and the chocolate in pieces, on the smaller one.

2 With beaten egg yolk, brush the pastry all round the mounds of filling. Lay the other sheet of pastry on top and seal the edges. Use a small, round, scalloped mould to cut out the tarts.

3 Brush each one with stiffly-whisked egg white and bake in a pre-heated oven at 200 °C / 400°F / Gas Mark 6 for 20 minutes. When the pastries are cooked, dust them with icing (confectioner's) sugar.

*To make the confectioner's custard, slowly bring half a litre (1 pint / 2¹/₂ cups) of milk to boiling point with 70 g (3 oz / 6 tbs.) granulated sugar, some lemon rind and a drop of vanilla essence. Beat 4 egg yolks with 60 g (2 oz / ³/₈ cup) granulated sugar, gradually folding in 2 tablespoons flour. Dilute with a drop of boiling milk, and add to the pan. Thicken for 10 min. over gentle heat, stirring with a whisk.*

# MUSTAZZOLA

Rich Fruit Tart

For the pastry:
400 g / 14 oz / 2 $^2/_3$ cups plain flour
150 g / 5 oz / $^3/_4$ cup granulated sugar
2 eggs
Milk
100 g / 4 oz / $^1/_2$ cup lard

For the filling:
100 g / 4 oz / $^1/_2$ cup honey
Almonds and hazelnuts, toasted
Walnut kernels
Half an orange
Plain flour
Ground cinnamon

Servings: 4
Preparation time: 40'+30'
Cooking time: 30'
Difficulty: ● ●
Kcal (per serving): 769
Proteins (per serving): 19
Fats (per serving): 43
Nutritional value: ● ● ●

Pile the flour into a heap on a pastry board and work in half a glass ($^1/_4$ cup) of milk. Make a smooth dough with the sugar, 80 g (3 oz / 6 tbs.) lard and the eggs. Roll into a ball and allow it to rest for half-an-hour. Dilute the honey in half a glass of water and pour into a small pan. Bring to the boil and gradually sprinkle in a tablespoon of flour, one handful of chopped almonds and one of chopped hazelnuts, a handful of walnut kernels, grated orange rind and a pinch of cinnamon.

Roll out the dough into a fairly thin sheet. Cut into 4- by 2-inch rectangles. At the centre of each, place a mound of the filling, and wrap the pastry diagonally around itself. Lay the *mustazzola* in an oven dish greased with lard and place in a pre-heated oven at 200 °C /400 °F / Gas Mark 6 for about half an hour.

# PIGNUCCATA

Fried Pastry Pine Cone

300 g / 11 oz / 2 cups plain flour
80 g / 3 oz / $^1/_3$ cup honey
80 g / 3 oz / 6 tbsp granulated sugar
3 egg yolks
Shelled almonds
Rind of half an orange
Ground cinnamon
Icing (confectioner's) sugar, optional
Oil for frying, salt

| | |
|---|---|
| Servings: | 4 |
| Preparation time: | 40'+30' |
| Cooking time: | 30' |
| Difficulty: | ●● |
| Kcal (per serving): | 943 |
| Proteins (per serving): | 20 |
| Fats (per serving): | 49 |
| Nutritional value: | ●●● |

Work the flour with the beaten egg yolks, adding the sugar and a pinch of salt, to make a smooth, elastic dough. Leave half an hour to rest. Divide into pieces which you will elongate with your hands to form long bread sticks. Cut into short lengths and fry in plenty of boiling hot oil. Drain and pile up into a pyramid on a serving plate. Keep hot.
Dilute the honey in half a glass of water and pour into a small pan with the finely-grated orange rind, a pinch of cinnamon and a handful of chopped almonds. Heat slowly, stirring well. When the honey has melted, pour it over the *pignuccata*. Dredge with icing (confectioner's) sugar, if you wish.

# RAVIOLI DI CARNALIVARI

Sweet Ravioli

Mix the flour with half a glass of water, working in the sugar, the lard, the beaten egg yolk and a drop of vanilla essence. When the dough is smooth and elastic, form it into a ball and leave for half an hour to rest. To make the filling, use a spatula to combine the sugar, grated lemon rind, a drop of vanilla essence, a pinch of cinnamon, a tablespoon of diced candied pumpkin and the crumbled chocolate with the ricotta. Blend well. Roll out the pastry thinly and cut into 6-inch squares. Pile a little of the filling to one side of each square, fold the other side over and trim the edges with the special instrument for making ravioli. Fry the pastry squares in plenty of boiling oil. When they have turned golden, drain them and dredge with icing (confectioner's) sugar.

**For the pastry:**
500 g / 1 lb 2 oz / 3 $^1$/$_3$ cup plain flour
100 g / 4 oz / $^1$/$_2$ cup granulated sugar
80 g / 3 oz / 6 tbsp lard (or butter)
1 egg yolk
Vanilla essence, icing (confectioner's) sugar
Oil for frying

**For the filling:**
450 g / 1 lb / 2$^1$/$_4$ cups fresh ricotta cheese
120 g / 5 oz / $^5$/$_8$ cup granulated sugar
Vanilla essence, half a lemon
Ground cinnamon
Candied pumpkin
Plain (semi-sweet) chocolate (half a bar)

| | |
|---|---|
| Servings: | 4 |
| Preparation time: | 1 h+30' |
| Cooking time: | 30' |
| Difficulty: | ●● |
| Kcal (per serving): | 1790 |
| Proteins (per serving): | 27 |
| Fats (per serving): | 104 |
| Nutritional value: | ●●● |

# SFOGGHIU

## Cheese Tart

**For the pastry:**
500 g / 1 lb 2 oz / 3 $^1/_3$ cups plain flour
3 egg yolks
150 g / 5 oz / $^3/_4$ cup granulated sugar
1 tsp lemon rind
80 g / 3 oz / 6 tbsp lard

**For the filling:**
150 g / 5 oz Sicilian toma (or any semi-fat cow's) cheese
80 g / 3 oz ricotta cheese
150 g / 5 oz / $^3/_4$ cup granulated sugar
2 egg whites
Plain (semi-sweet) chocolate, (half a bar)
Cinnamon
Candied pumpkin and glacé cherries

| | |
|---|---|
| Servings: 4 | |
| Preparation time: 45'+5-6 h | |
| Cooking time: 30' | |
| Difficulty: ● ● ● | |
| Kcal (per serving): 1539 | |
| Proteins (per serving): 38 | |
| Fats (per serving): 70 | |
| Nutritional value: ● ● ● | |

1 Prepare the filling by mixing the finely-sliced toma cheese, a tablespoon of diced candied pumpkin, a handful of glacé cherries (roughly chopped), the crumbled chocolate, the sugar and a teaspoon of ground cinnamon. Amalgamate it all with the stiffly-whipped egg whites. Leave to rest for 5-6 hours.

2 Knead the flour with a little water, the lard, sugar, grated lemon rind and beaten egg yolks. When the dough is nice and even, leave to rest half an hour. Roll out the pastry and line an oven dish, allowing it to drop over the sides. Pour in the filling, level it off, fold the edges over and bake in the oven at 160 °C / 300 °F / Gas Mark 2 for about half an hour. When the surface turns golden, take out and serve.

# ZIPPULI

## Fried Rice Fingers

400 g / 14 oz / 1²/₃ cups rice
120 g / 4 oz / ³/₄ cup flour
100 g / 4 oz / ¹/₂ cup
  granulated sugar
¹/₂ l / 1 pt / 2 ¹/₂ cups milk
15 g / 0.6 oz fresh brewer's
  yeast or 2 ¹/₄ tsp active dry
  yeast
Half an orange, cinnamon
Icing (confectioner's) sugar
Oil for frying

| | |
|---|---|
| **Servings:** 4 | |
| **Preparation time:** 40'+2 h | |
| **Cooking time:** 45' | |
| **Difficulty:** ● ● | |
| **Kcal (per serving):** 888 | |
| **Proteins (per serving):** 14 | |
| **Fats (per serving):** 30 | |
| **Nutritional value:** ● ● ● | |

1 Boil the rice in the milk. Draw off the heat and allow to cool. Stir in the flour, 50 g (2 oz / ¹/₄ cup) granulated sugar, a little ground cinnamon, the yeast and a teaspoon of finely-grated orange rind. Mix well until the dough is quite thick. Leave 2 hours to rise.

2 Roll the dough out on a pastry board to a thickness of half-an-inch. Cut out long bread sticks half-an-inch wide. Fry them in plenty of boiling oil in a frying pan. When the *zippuli* turn golden, drain them and dust with icing (confectioner's) sugar.

127

*Stampato presso il*
*Centro Stampa Editoriale Bonechi*
*Sesto Fiorentino - Firenze*